Never Fear
Your Climb

Keep Climbing
Kylee ♡
Culbine

Keep Climbing ♥ life ~ Alexis

Never Fear Your Climb

How I Turned My Tragedy Into A Survival Guide

Kylee Cubine

HIGH BRIDGE BOOKS

HOUSTON

Never Fear Your Climb
by Kylee Cubine

Printed in the United States of America
ISBN (Paperback): 978-1-946615-76-3
ISBN (Hardcover): 978-1-946615-42-8

High Bridge Books titles may be purchased in bulk for educational, busi-ness, fundraising, or sales promotional use. For information, please con-tact High Bridge Books via www.HighBridgeBooks.com/contact.

Published in Houston, Texas by High Bridge Books.

Contents

1

What If?

HAVE YOU EVER THOUGHT ABOUT THE WHAT-IFS in life? What if I had this or that? What if this had happened to me or that had never happened to me? What if this day had turned out differently?

My what-if happened when I was 13 years old and in the eighth grade. What if I'd had club volleyball practice on the evening of Sunday, January 20, 2013?

I am an only child and have the most amazing parents a girl could ask for. I am so thankful to have them. I loved spending time with my family and friends. I loved being outside and playing all kinds of sports, but my favorite was soccer, which I've played since I was four years old.

I was a pretty normal 13-year-old. My weekdays consisted of school all day, practicing whatever sport I had going on at school, and then club soccer practice in the evening. My weekends usually consisted of soccer tournaments on both Saturday and Sunday. If we didn't have a tournament on Sunday, I spent the morning at church and the evening with family or friends. I lived a very busy lifestyle and was always on the go. I like to think that I am a very hard worker at whatever I am doing, whether that be school, sports, or even helping others.

Sunday, January 20, 2013, was a normal day that was supposed to consist of church in the morning and then volleyball practice for my new club team in the evening. However, I did not realize my world as it existed would come to a complete stop and set me on a new journey for the next several years.

We'd had a long day the day before and decided to stay home from church that Sunday. We rested that morning and spent time doing chores around the house. Around noon, we got a message that volleyball practice had been canceled for the day and would be rescheduled during the week. I was relieved to have a break to rest, but I had gotten a message from my cousin Danielle to ride in my uncle's ATVs. I agreed because I hadn't had much free time to spend time with my family, and ever since I was little, this is what my cousins and I did when I wasn't busy.

My dad dropped me off. We started riding as soon as I got there. We always took turns driving the ATVs. Around three o'clock in the afternoon, it was Danielle's turn to drive, so I moved over to the passenger seat, and let her get into the driver seat. When Danielle took off going down a slight hill, we thought it would be a good idea to get a snack from the house.

She was going slow when I said she should tell her friend on the other ATV where we were going, in case she wanted to follow us or wanted us to bring her something back. Little did I know my whole life was about to change in the next couple of seconds. When we turned around, we flipped. Danielle was thrown out in front of the ATV, while I was still inside. I checked to make sure Danielle was okay, but she got up and started walking around as if everything was fine.

I then checked myself to make sure I was okay; little did I know this was about to be the moment that would change my life and cause it to come to a complete stop. I noticed one of my sweatpant legs was up, and when I put my leg out, I saw it was wide open to where you could see the bone. At that moment, I thought I must be dreaming and would wake up any minute. I looked down at my leg and could not imagine how any doctor could fix this. I had watched every episode of *Grey's Anatomy* and had never seen this happen on there. I have seen a lot of bad injuries before, but nothing like this. How could anyone fix my leg? I began thinking the doctors would have to amputate it.

My uncle Ricky, Danielle's grandpa, was riding his ATV when he noticed we had flipped, and he rushed over to us. He could see Danielle screaming, jumping up and down, and crying for him to come quickly. Before he got to me, he thought I was dead because I wasn't making a sound or crying. When he realized I was still alive, he immediately took a deep breath. He then called 911 and my parents, as I sat there in the ATV hoping this was all just a dream.

When my parents finally arrived, I was still sitting inside the ATV, waiting for the ambulance to arrive. I was so thankful my parents arrived before the ambulance because I was not going anywhere without my mom. She rushed over to me, and the first thing I did was put my hand on her shoulder and ask if I would be able to play soccer again. My mom had no idea what to say, but she told me everything would be okay.

After what felt like forever, the ambulance, finally showed up to take me to the emergency room. The paramedics got my leg all wrapped up and started to load me into the ambulance. Then it hit me. I had never been in an ambulance nor had I ever been to the emergency room.

After about ten minutes, we finally arrived at the hospital's emergency room. I was put into a room, where nurses started coming in like crazy to take care of me. As I laid there, they started cutting my favorite sweatpants off. Hey, I know this isn't a big deal because they were trying to save my leg, but everyone has their favorite pieces of clothing. I was still in shock with everything going on around me and was hoping this was just a bad dream that I would wake up from at any second.

The doctor on call came in to start cleaning all the dirt from my leg. I was so in shock that I hadn't felt pain until he started pouring large amounts of solution on it to flush it out. As I screamed in pain, nurses rushed into my room to see what was going on. The on-call doctor was sending pictures to a family friend of ours who was the orthopedic surgeon at the hospital, Dr. Fontenot.

When Dr. Fontenot arrived, he pulled my parents out into the hallway and told them that I was like a daughter to him, and if I stayed at Longview, I would lose my leg. He explained that the hospital did not have the kind of equipment or technology needed to save my leg. My parents immediately asked what they needed to do to help me. Dr. Fontenot said not to worry about a thing because he already had a helicopter from Dallas Children's Medical center on the way to get me.

When my parents came back into the room and told me what the plan was, I still felt this was all a dream. I wasn't even worried about my leg anymore—now all I was thinking about was flying in a helicopter. I'd never flown anywhere in my life, and now they wanted me to get into a helicopter. I was freaking out because my mom wouldn't be with me. I told Dr. Fontenot I was not going anywhere without my mom, and they could just drive me to Dallas themselves. He told me not to worry about a thing. He'd told the other hospital to send the biggest helicopter they had so my mom could ride with me.

The flight crew arrived and began to wrap my leg so it would be stable for the flight to Dallas. When this crew shows up, they take over completely and take the best care of children until they land on the air pad at Dallas Children's Medical Center. After about 10 minutes of preparing me for the flight and helping me get some relief from pain, it was time to go.

After 45 minutes, we finally arrived at Dallas Children's Medical Center, and they took me straight into a room. After finally calming down from the flight, the nurses began talking about how to get me ready for surgery. The minute I heard the word surgery, the nervousness came back because I'd never had surgery before—another "first" in my life.

Two doctors came into the room to assess my leg. One was an orthopedic doctor, and the other was a plastics doctor. They evaluated my leg and said I would also need a vascular doctor to make sure my vascular supply was still intact. My dad finally arrived by vehicle right before I was about to go into surgery for the first time.

While I was laying in the room, waiting to go back to the operating room and answering the nurse's questions, I realized I had to go to the bathroom. I was lying in a hospital bed—how in the world was I supposed to get up with my leg wide open and walk to the bathroom?

When I told my mom I needed to go to the bathroom, one of the nurses heard me and said, "You need to go to the bathroom? Okay, that's no problem; let me go get you a pan."

I said to my mom, "I have to go to the bathroom in a cooking pan," and everyone in the room began to laugh.

The nurse said, "No, sweetheart, it's a bathroom bedpan that patients use when they cannot move from the bed."

At that moment, for just a few seconds, everything seemed so calm and normal, and I wasn't thinking about surgery. But the moment passed, and I was back to worrying about experiencing another scary thing in my life. After using the bathroom pan, not a cooking pan, it was time to go to the operating room.

After being in the operating room for seven hours, I woke up in recovery, realizing this was all real and nothing was going change for quite some time. The doctors came around and told my parents and me what was wrong with my leg. They told us that my tibia, one of the long bones in the lower leg, was broken in three places and that the skin in that entire area had been degloved. That means that when my bone broke, it had nowhere to go due to the tension, so it went through my skin, causing a compound fracture. They said they had to put a temporary external fixator on my leg until they could get all the dirt out during many future surgeries to come in the next several days.

My vascular doctor came in and told me that everything was intact. All the doctors said I needed to be ready because I had a long road ahead of me. Sitting there after waking up from surgery and hearing the doctors' diagnosis had me in shock. How could this have happened to me? At that moment, I questioned everything about God and my faith. I just could not understand how he allowed this to happen to me.

I went to church, I stayed out of trouble, I did what I was taught, I respected others, and I always worked hard. I sat back and began to explore all the reasons this could have happened to me, out of all people. Was this a time for me to grow closer to God? Don't get me wrong—we went to church on Sundays and believed in God, but we also went through the motions a lot. We didn't mean to, but our lives were crazy busy with my parents working so hard and the time invested in getting me to school and sports. I honestly had no idea what to think any more about my faith and God, and I just wanted to question everything. All I knew at this moment was that I had a long road ahead of me and didn't know where it would lead me. The question that popped into my head at that moment was, "What if I had just had volleyball practice?"

This is me in eighth grade at 13 years old, right before my accident.

These are my parents, Robert and Angel Cubine. They are my number-one supporters in everything I do.

This is my cousin, Danielle Taylor. We were inseparable growing up over the years.

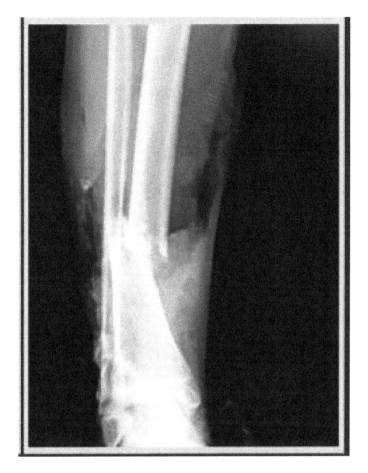

This is the first X-ray taken of my leg right after the accident.

2

Reality Sets In

REALITY STARTED TO SINK IN AFTER THE DOCTORS told me everything that was wrong with my leg. I began to realize that nothing was going to change. I wasn't going to wake up from a bad dream, and this was my life, for who knew how long. The doctors had said before they could begin repairing my leg, I needed at least four more surgeries that consisted of just cleaning all the dirt so I wouldn't get an infection. They were still concerned that, even being the specialists they were and with the technology available, they probably still wouldn't be able to save my leg.

The next few days and nights in the hospital were so long. I couldn't sleep, I was in pain, and I was away from home. I was two hours away from all my friends and family, which made it hard for my friends to visit all the time. However, I still had tons of visitors, and I will forever be grateful for them.

I was unable to attend school, of course, so I had to withdraw until I was able to go again. The principal said if I missed all those days, I would have to stay back a year and wouldn't be able to graduate with my class. I did not like the idea of that. I grew up with all those people and wanted to graduate with them.

After being in the hospital for a week, I was exhausted and just ready to go home. I had five surgeries that week and was unable to have food every night for 12 hours because of the next surgery. However, even when I was out of surgery, I did not feel like eating because I was so sick from the anesthesia. I started to become very skinny and pale. My mom and dad watched me suffer every night in pain, and they were unable to do anything to help. I was already on high-level pain medication.

One night during that week, a nurse walking by heard me crying from being in so much pain, so she came into my room. She asked my mom why I wasn't on a pain pump. The nurse then asked my doctor if they could put me on one, and he said yes. The pain pump was a button I could push to give me pain medicine whenever the button lit up. I knew the minute they began to hook up the pain pump that button and I were going to be best friends.

At the end of the week, the doctors told me I was getting close to having the big surgery to repair my leg. I needed one more small surgery, my sixth one, so they could put a camera in my leg and see what they needed to do before the big surgery. Surgery number seven would take place on January 29—my 14th birthday. They told me just to rest for the next few days. Rest. I didn't even know what that word meant anymore. How could I rest when all I would be thinking about was my big, scary surgery? They also wanted me to try to eat, but I still couldn't because even after five surgeries, I was still feeling sick.

During the first week at the hospital, I received many gifts and candy from all the visitors. My hospital room could have been another gift shop for the hospital. While I was resting up for those next few days, my dad helped me sort out all of my candy. I stored some of it in a cabinet for myself. The rest I placed in another cabinet to share with my nurses, other nurses on my floor, the kids on my floor, and their family members.

It was soon time for the small surgery where they would put the camera in my leg. Although this surgery wasn't that serious, I was still scared because I would still have to be put to sleep—again. When I woke up from surgery and went back to my room the next day, I saw a roomful of gifts that the hospital and my parents had gotten me for my fourteenth birthday. They also got me a cookie cake to celebrate.

I had to lay flat for the next four hours to reduce the chance of serious bleeding, so that's how I celebrated my birthday—lying flat. I began to open the gifts. I opened a singing birthday card from my mom and dad. It sang "The Climb" by Miley Cyrus. Before my accident, this song was just another song to me, but while lying in the hospital bed listening, it became everything to me. The lyrics hit home. From that moment on, my journey was about making my climb to the top of the mountain to see the view on the other side.

Twelve o'clock finally came, and I was unable to eat once again, but, hey, it was my big day. I'm not talking about my birthday, as most kids would have been excited about; however, I knew that the moment the surgery began at seven that morning and ended that night, I would be one step closer to getting back on that soccer field.

The doctors came in that morning to explain the procedure. They were going to take an entire muscle, called latissimus dorsi, from my back and put it in my leg. This is called a muscle flap graft. This would leave a ten-inch scar on my back. They were also going to take skin from my thigh, which is called a skin graft. I thought I was nervous before, but now I was scared out of my mind. This surgery would last 12 hours, and it was on my birthday. You know how everyone has that birthday they wish they can forget about? Well, I knew this would be that birthday for me, but, hey, who could say they got to sleep all day on their birthday? Yes, it would just be the anesthesia keeping me asleep, but I preferred to look on the bright side.

After 12 hours, my mom and dad, who were in the waiting room, finally got the call that I was out of surgery. My mom looked down at her phone at that moment and saw that it was 7:34 p.m. What's crazy about that is it was the exact same time I was born 14 years ago on that day. It also had been storming all day when I was born, and it was also storming all day while I was in surgery. I started to realize that God was trying to make us realize that he was still in charge and there with us always, even though I was still so unsure of my faith.

When I arrived in the ICU room, they moved me to another bed, where I would stay for the next few days. After already not being able to eat 12 hours before my surgery, the nurse told me I couldn't eat for another 36 hours after this surgery. This was because they had to make sure my skin graft took. If it didn't, I had to be ready to go back into surgery again, with nothing in my belly, so as not to aspirate.

Over the past nine days, whenever I was unable to eat or drink, my parents didn't eat or drink either. But since I couldn't eat for the next 36 hours, I had to allow my parents to eat. They each took turns going out so they would not eat in front of me. I hated being in the ICU and was just ready to get out of there. All I wanted the whole time I was unable to eat or drink was a cold Pepsi.

One afternoon in ICU, I encountered a nurse practitioner who wasn't one of my favorite people in the world. I had been in the hospital for 10 days by now, and I had been unable to get out of bed. Because I had been lying flat, I had a sore on my bottom. During the day, the nurse practitioner came in and said she needed to have a look at the sore and wanted to move me on my side to avoid putting pressure on that spot. We told the nurse practitioner that I had a muscle from my back removed, with a 10-inch incision and a pain pump placed in this area, so please be careful lifting me.

The nurse practitioner and another nurse lifted me up, and the nurse practitioner put her hands under my back right where I had just had surgery. I started yelling and crying because it hurt so bad, and all I wanted was to be put down. I told my mom right after they put me down and left that I did not want that person back in my room. My mom told my nurse to make sure she didn't come back.

The next day, the nurse practitioner stood outside my ICU room and asked for my mom and dad to come outside. She said, "I would just like to apologize for my actions yesterday."

My mom said, "The person you should be talking to is that girl right there lying in that bed." My mom and dad walked back into my room and said, "Someone would like to speak to you."

The nurse practitioner walked in and apologized to me. I told her that it was okay and thanked her for her apology.

I didn't sleep at all the whole time I was in the ICU and just wanted to get to a normal room. When I was finally allowed to have food and drink, I knew I was getting closer to moving to a normal room. The doctors finally came in and told me that I could be moved into a room, but it would be a different room with different nurses. This was scary to me because I had become so close to the nurses I had before the big surgery.

However, I was just glad to be moving to a normal room and out of the ICU. When I arrived in my new room, I saw an amazing view of the Dallas skyline. My parents, however, were not a fan of the couch bed because it wasn't as big as the previous couch bed. They had not left my side once during the two weeks we had been in the hospital.

The next morning, the doctors came in for rounds and told me it was time to start healing, and I had a long road ahead of me. I didn't believe it would be that long of a road. I thought to myself, *Well, if I work hard in therapy and do everything they tell me, I can be back out playing soccer in no time.* Boy, I was sure wrong about that one! They also told me I could eat whatever I wanted if my parents got it for me.

I had many visitors during this time. It was still hard though because I was so used to being with my friends 24/7, and now I could only see them whenever they didn't have school. Although many were unable to come see me, I knew I had so many more people back home praying and thinking of me. That meant the world to me. Many people started fundraisers for my parents and me. My parents both took off work and stayed with me the entire time I was in the hospital. God truly blessed me with amazing parents because they never once left my side during this time.

I also had my amazing BB and Papaw, who are my grandparents on my dad's side. They came to visit me all the time. Unfortunately, my other grandparents on my mom's side were unable to come visit me often. My grandma Mimi was very ill and always in pain, and I was two hours away from her.

Cleaning and dressing my leg became a big part of my days after the big surgery. The doctors and nurses would come in and redress my leg, and my mom, being a nurse, watched and learned what they were doing. About a week or so after the big surgery, it was time to take the staples out of my leg that they had put in to make sure the skin graft stayed. I hated the idea of them pulling staples out of my leg, so we called my child life specialist to the room to hold my hand.

A child life specialist is a person assigned to a child when they enter the Children's Hospital to help make sure they are okay mentally and be there when they are scared or want someone to talk to. My child life specialist was named Mary Catharine, and she was amazing. She was always there when I needed her throughout the day. Anytime I had to do anything scary like get my staples out, she was always there. She always held my hand and talked me through it. She also made sure I wasn't picking at my lip because that's what I do when I'm nervous about something. My lips became very sore during my hospital stay.

The doctors came in every morning for rounds, checked my leg, and asked how I was doing and if I was eating a lot. One day they said I should get in the wheelchair and go explore the hospital since I'd been stuck in my room since I arrived. Although I was not up for it, I thought it might make me feel better to get out of this room and see something other than four walls I'd looked at for what seemed like forever. They brought in a wheelchair, I got in with my leg sticking straight out in a parallel position, and we went around the hospital.

You wouldn't think there would be much to look at in a hospital, but this was not just any hospital. It had amazing views of Dallas from my floor, and downstairs was an amazing train track—the thing was huge. After being out of my room for almost 30 minutes, I was looking at the trains and started to feel sick. I told my mom I thought I was about to throw up, and she said it was probably from the motion of the elevator going up and down. I knew that meant it was time to go back to the room.

Days went by, and my mom, my dad, and I started to get the hang of life in the hospital. My mom and I figured out how to wash my hair and bathe me all while laying down and not being able to move my leg. I started getting used to the doctors coming in and making rounds between six and eight in the morning. I thought being in the hospital would at least allow me to sleep late.

I started learning what hospital foods I liked the most. It wasn't hard to like the food because it was amazing. I know you're probably wondering how hospital food could be good, but, trust me, it was like getting food from a five-star restaurant. The hospital cooks should open their own restaurant.

My dad figured out how to lift me onto the bathroom pan without hurting the incision on my back. My mom also learned how to clean and dress my leg, so every time the nurses came in, my mom already had it done. Last, but not least, we all finally learned what the word rest meant. With all the weeks of restless nights, it felt good to finally start sleeping through the night. I was able to keep my pain down so I could rest. Life in the hospital became the new normal for us at the time.

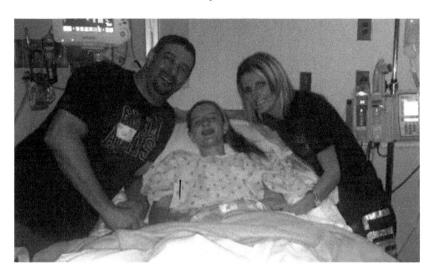

We started taking a family picture before each surgery, and this was the first one we ever took.

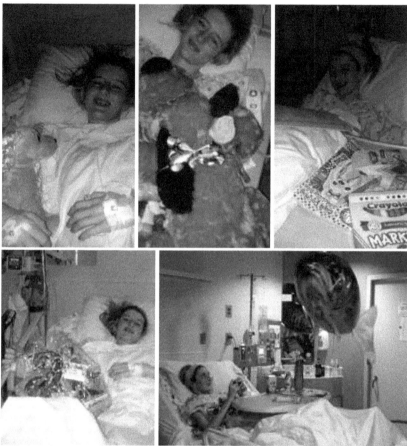

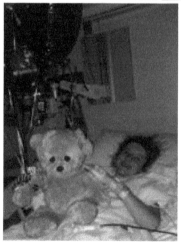

This is just a small amount of the gifts I received while I was in the hospital room. The gifts, cards, candy, and even the people that came by all touched my heart in ways I will never be able to describe. I also will never be able to thank each of you enough. I also received probably over a thousand birthday and get-well-soon cards from people in my school and town.

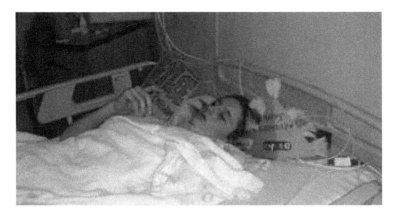

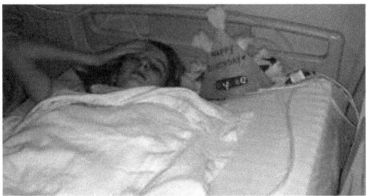

*This is my 14th birthday party that was thrown in the hospital
room the night before my big surgery and actual birthday.*

The amazing nurses on my floor and my parents got me gifts, a cookie cake, and lots of sweets.

This is the singing card from my parents that sang "The Climb" by Miley Cyrus. It started my journey of climbing to the top of my mountain.

These are my grandparents on my mom's side who I call Papa and Mimi.

These are my grandparents on my dad's side who I call BB and Papaw.

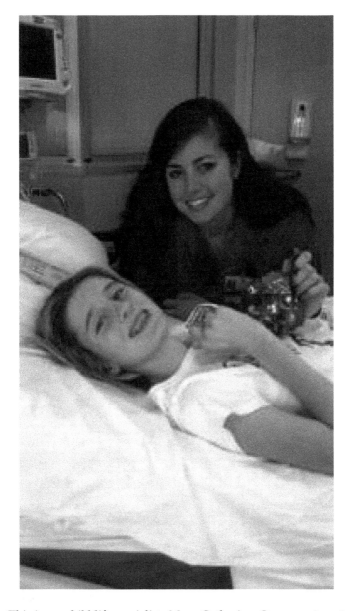

This is my child life specialist, Mary Catharine. Over my stay at the hospital, she became one of my favorite people to talk to. She and I became best friends, and I will never be able to repay her for everything she did for me.

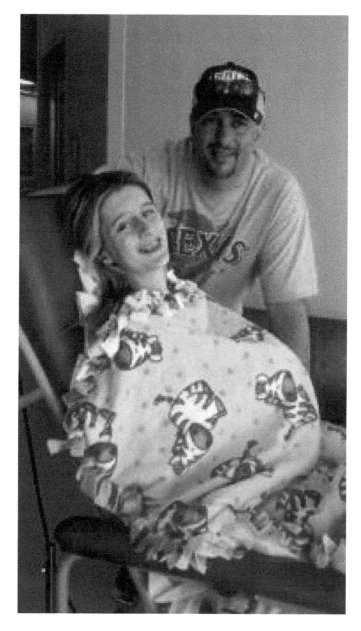

This is the very first time I was able to get out of the hospital bed and move around the hospital floor. As you can see, I am not feeling up to it.

3

Kindred Blessings

I COULDN'T HAVE DONE MY STAY AT THE HOSPITAL without my amazing family and friends who stayed by my side from the beginning. My parents would tell me that God himself also helped me keep my courage and strength, but it was still hard for me to wrap my head around everything. I'm not saying I didn't believe in God anymore, but I was questioning how he could let this happen to me.

So many visitors came and went, but it was still hard on the days when no one came. It was nice to have those days, but at the same time, it made me realize I was two hours away from home. Friends had school, and others had work, and I was stuck in this lonely hospital.

Even though I was two hours from home, I could still feel the love, even on the days when I had no visitors. There is this amazing thing called social media. I was able to see everyone who was keeping up with my story and praying for me. I had so many people texting me and posting on my social media accounts, telling me they were praying for me. The night I was hurt, I did not have my phone, and the next morning when I woke up from surgery, my mom gave me my phone back. I had 300 text messages and about 30 phone calls with people telling me they were thinking of me and praying for me.

What I love about social media is that people can stay connected no matter the distance. I was able to see what all my friends were up to, and it made me feel like I was right there with them.

Many people reached out to me who I didn't even know. They had heard my story from someone else or saw it on Facebook. Most people my age do not realize the power of prayer, and I didn't either until I saw how many people were praying for me. I would get messages on Facebook from someone who knew someone that I knew, saying they were praying for me, and I was so thankful for that. It was amazing how something so terrible like a 13-year-old girl from a small town being hurt in an ATV wreck could bring so many people toward God. These little things increased my faith. I knew there had to be a reason why this happened to me but hadn't found it yet. Just seeing all these people come together to pray was one of the many reasons my faith in God began to be restored. However, this was still just the beginning of my journey with God.

I was so excited when visitors came, especially my best friend Maleah and some of my other friends. We played board games, they would do my hair and nails, or we would just laugh and talk. When it was time for them to go, I was sad. I was truly thankful that I had visitors, but it was just hard because I realized they were heading back home two hours away, and I had to stay in a hospital bed for who knew how much longer.

Throughout the whole time I was in the hospital, not only did I have amazing visitors, but I also had amazing doctors and nurses. I loved all my nurses very much, but there were two I have continued a friendship with. One was a daytime nurse, and the other was a nighttime nurse.

My daytime nurse was Jon Higginbotham. He always knew how to make me laugh when I was having a bad day. Anytime he walked into my room, I would start smiling because I knew he was about to say something funny to make me feel better. One day I was telling my mom and dad my back was itching, and I couldn't reach it. Jon walked in as I was telling my mom I needed a back scratcher. We had pillowcases that we let the nurses and doctors sign, and Jon wrote on the pillowcase, "Kylee, you are so awesome and strong! I can't wait to see you run and shoot and excel in life! Here is the back scratcher you always wanted! Love, Jon." He drew a back scratcher on the pillowcase.

The day before my big surgery when I came out from the small surgery, Jon was in my room with a hat he had made that said, "Happy Birthday, Kylee." We have stayed in touch with Jon ever since the accident. He was a big part of my hospital stay and my journey. I will forever be thankful for Jon.

My nighttime nurse was Amber Hunter. She always knew how to come into my room at night and give me the medicine I needed in my IV without waking me up. She also knew that if I was sleeping, I was not in pain, so she wouldn't wake me to ask if I needed pain medicine. She knew I was finally getting some rest. Every time she walked into my room to start her shift, I would get so excited because I knew she was my nurse for the night. I also offered her candy every time that it was a long night.

Amber always came into my room before leaving to tell me good morning and that she would see me later. One night had been particularly long because I'd been in pain all night. I asked her where she was going and why she couldn't stay, and she said, "It's time for me to go home, girl, and go to sleep." I pointed to the pull-out couch my parents slept on and told her there was a bed right there she could sleep on. She smiled and gave me a big hug. Amber and I stay in touch to this day. We visit with each other almost every time I'm in Dallas for doctors' visits or just there hanging out. I love Amber so very much and will forever be thankful for her.

Like I said before, many people reached out to me through Facebook who I didn't know. One day my mom got a message from Amber Hapka, who said that she had heard about my story through a friend and wanted to reach out to us. Her husband, Mark Hapka, had a serious ATV wreck a few years before mine, and she and her husband wanted to come talk to me about his wreck and show me that if you don't give up and have faith, you can be restored.

At first, my mom was a little worried because they were strangers, but she told them they could visit. It was too late to see me the night they arrived because visiting hours were over. My dad went down to meet them and introduce himself. When he came back up to the room, he had cupcakes that Amber and Mark had brought me. My dad told my mom and me that they were nice people and that they were going to come back and visit.

The next day, when they walked into the room, I was a little nervous because I'm kind of shy when it comes to meeting new people. But after a while, I started to warm up. Mark showed me pictures of the injuries from his ATV wreck. He asked what I liked to do, and I told him I love to play soccer. He said he loved to run marathons and that he had just finished running that morning.

After seeing the pictures of his injuries, I was amazed that he was even walking again. He said he worked for the

Dallas Mavericks and even showed me the ring the people who work there got when they won. He let me put it on my finger, and it was the coolest thing. We talked about various things, and before you knew it, it was like we had known them forever.

Mark and Amber were a huge reason I never gave up. They continue to help push me through it all and have become lifelong family friends. It's crazy that at that moment in time, I was wondering how I would get through it all, and God brought angels into my life to help at just the right time. I had been wondering why this accident had to happen to me, and when I met Mark and Amber, I realized they were one of the reasons it did. If the accident hadn't happened, I would have never met them. They showed me how I could reach out to others and encourage them not to give up as well. I will forever be thankful for Mark and Amber Hapka and will love them forever.

Another family that helped me through a lot while I was in the hospital and continue to help me to this day is the Gees, James and Heather. Heather had a daughter named Sophie Steelman, who is one of my best friends. We met them about six months before my accident. Sophie and I played on the same club soccer team. Over those six months before my accident, we had become close to them, and our families did everything together. We also had Texas Roadhouse every Tuesday night after soccer practice.

Heather had another daughter named Sydnee Steelman, and James had two children of his own, named Trinity and Cole. They all became like the siblings I never had. When I got hurt the night of my accident and went to the emergency room in Longview, they dropped everything and rushed right to me. Sophie was at her dad's that night, and he rushed her to me. When I got ready to fly out to Dallas that night, James and Heather went with my dad back to our house to pack up a few things. They all then rushed to Dallas to be with me.

Throughout the whole time I was in the hospital, they always came to visit. They helped my parents with anything they needed and did the same for me. I will always love this family more than they will ever know. They will always mean the world to me, and I will forever be thankful for all the things they have done and continue to do for me.

One person I cannot leave out is my cousin, Danielle Taylor. She is my cousin on my mom's side and was driving when we had our ATV wreck. Even though I am the one who got hurt in the wreck physically, Danielle was hurt mentally. For the longest time, she blamed herself for what happened to me. She always told me she was so sorry. The word flew fast around our school, and that didn't help either, as everyone would ask her how it happened and how I was doing.

I was glad everyone was concerned about me, but I also wished people had made sure Danielle was okay because she was driving the ATV the time of the accident. She didn't have injuries, but she did blame herself for my injury. Every time Danielle came to visit, I told her to stop blaming herself and that it was an accident and could have happened to anyone. Danielle and I have grown extremely close through this accident. She is an amazing human being and will always mean the world to me. I love her to death and thank her always for being there for me through it all.

My friends, family, and role models mean everything to me. They are one of the many reasons I'm where I am today. They lifted my spirits when I needed it most. You find out who your true friends are through something like this. You find out who's going to take time out of their day to make sure you're okay. Life brings you challenges, which determine who comes out on the other side. Along the way, you realize those who are there for you and those who mean the most.

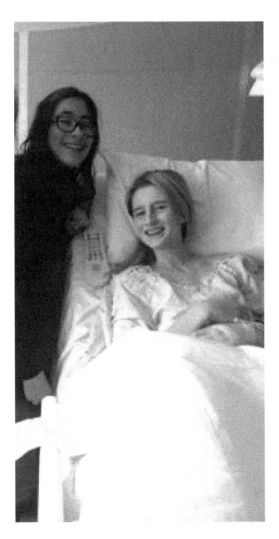

This is Maleah, one of my best friends. We have been best friends since seventh grade.

This is my day nurse from Dallas Children's Medical Center, Jon Higginbotham. He never failed to make me laugh when I was having a bad day.

This is my night nurse from Dallas Children's Medical Center, Amber Hunter. She never left a shift without saying goodbye to me.

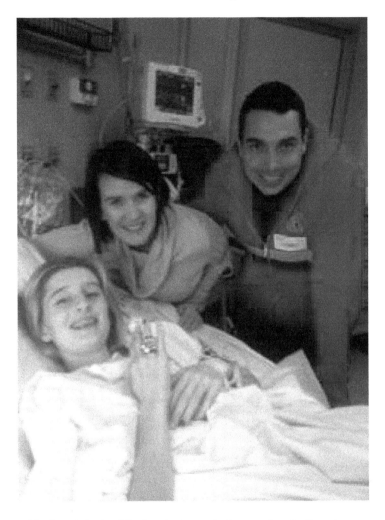

Mark and Amber Hapka, the two who became inspirations to me the minute I met them

James and Heather Gee, Trinity Gee, Sydnee Steelman, Sophie Steelman, and Cole Gee (clockwise from top left). I'm so thankful to have had a family like this in my life at the time of my accident.

Danielle came to visit me as much as she could while I was in the hospital, and it was nice. After the accident, we became even closer as cousins.

4

No Place Like Home

AFTER BEING IN THE HOSPITAL FOR ALMOST A month and not seeing the outside world other than through a window, we finally got the news that I could be discharged and finish my long recovery at home. The doctors told me the only reason they were letting me go home this early was that my mom was a nurse and knew what she was doing when it came to cleaning and bandaging my leg, and we had the whole dangling process down as well. They said that they wanted to see me once a week for a doctor's visit. This would become our usual for quite some time.

We packed everything up and got ready to head home the next day. I was so excited to be able to go home, but I was nervous at the same time. When it was time to leave, we loaded everything up in the car and headed home. That ride home was the longest car ride ever. I hadn't been in a car for almost a month, and I was getting sick every five minutes.

We finally made it home after a three-hour car ride, whereas it normally takes us two hours to get home from Dallas. I was relieved to be home, knowing I would be sleeping under my own roof. When I pulled up to the house, my Mimi and Papa, who lived behind us, came to see me. I couldn't be happier to see them. Being in the hospital was the longest I had ever gone without seeing my grandparents.

We set up a little sleeping area for me to sleep in the living room because the bed in my room was too tall for me to be getting in and out of. Also, being in a wheelchair didn't help because my bed took up almost all my room. Also, my parents' room was closer to the living room, just in case I needed them during the night, and this gave me comfort and made me at ease.

The living room became my new bedroom for a while. Everything that I was so used to doing on my own, I now needed someone to help me. I needed my mom to help me take showers. I had to have my mom or dad to bring me food and drink when needed. I'm not complaining because it was nice sometimes, but you never realize how blessed you are to simply walk into the kitchen and make a plate of food or get a snack until your independence is taken away from you.

You don't realize how blessed you are to simply go to the bathroom by yourself until you are no longer able to do this small task on your own. I had now upgraded from the "cooking pan" to using the bathroom in the living room in a bedside bathroom chair because my leg was unable to drop down from a parallel position, and it was hard to fit the wheelchair into the bathrooms. My parents also had to bring me my toothbrush and a bucket to spit in to brush my teeth in the living room. I went from being an independent kid, who did everything by themselves, to needing help with almost everything I did.

I was still unable to go to school because my leg had to stay straight all the time. My mom was working with the school to help get me in Homebound. Homebound is like homeschool, except the school sent a teacher to my house to bring my school work and help me get it done.

Even though I was home, it just did not feel the same as before. I needed help with everything, I was unable to attend school, and I was unable to practice the sports I had partici-pated in. Don't get me wrong though—I loved being home. Although I was not able to practice, I still went to all my soc-cer practices just to get out of the house and stay involved. You would think I would be sick of Dallas, but I wanted to be there to support my club soccer team, so every weekend I tried my hardest to be there. Most of the time, we would get lucky and be able to schedule my doctor appointments on Friday and stay in a hotel that night to watch them play on Saturday.

One good thing about being home was my friends and visitors could visit me more often because I was closer. Some friends would even stay the night sometimes. We had so many visitors during those first few weeks that I lost count. We numerous people help us during that time who we will forever be grateful for. Tons of people even brought us lunches and dinners.

Another thing that was good about being home was that I got my puppy, Zendaya—a miniature Yorkie. Before my accident, we had picked her out but were unable to get her because her litter was not ready to be taken away from their mom. When we got home, I kept asking my mom if we could please bring her home, and she said we couldn't. It turned out that when we got home from the hospital, my mom had gotten permission for us to bring her home, but she tricked me and said no because she wanted to surprise me.

Two days later, my mom and dad drove about an hour to get Zendaya, and I stayed at home with my grandparents on my dad's side, BB and Papaw. The minute they brought that dog home, we became best friends. She would sleep by my leg and make sure no one hurt it, even though she weighed like a pound. I love that dog so much because she came to me in a time where I needed someone to keep a smile on my face.

It was finally time for my dad to go back to work, but my mom stayed home with me for a little longer. It was hard to get used to him not being there during the day. If my mom and I wanted to go somewhere or had to run an errand, it was harder because my mom had to help get me into the car and then load my wheelchair in the back. An errand that usually took 20 minutes took about 40 minutes.

Not only did it take long, but everywhere I went, someone would stop me and ask what happened. After a while, it started to get tiring, so I asked my mom if I could make flyers stating what happened to me and hand one to everyone who asked. Not only was it hard to go places, but it was hard to stay home. Can you just imagine having a teenage girl and her mom in a house by themselves together during the day? Some days I would break down crying because I couldn't do anything by myself and would want to give up.

One day, I literally just broke down crying and told everyone that I was done trying. I went to another room in the house and sat in my wheelchair thinking about everything. I was still unsure why this had happened to me, but as I sat there in silence, it all hit me. Instead of saying *why me,* I started saying *why not me?* I never in a million years would wish this injury on anyone else, to endure the pain I had over those past few weeks or would in the years to come.

I knew my relationship with God was nowhere close to where I wanted it to be. I just didn't know how to grow closer to God. I was only 14 and was starting to develop my own opinions. I needed a little kick in the butt to make me realize that I could grow closer to God and, along the way, help others grow closer to God as well. God didn't intentionally hurt me, but he gave me this path—or as I like to say—this mountain to overcome and grow closer to him. I knew at that moment I was going to stop all the what-ifs and start looking at everything from a different perspective. Without this accident, I wouldn't have learned so many things about myself. I sat there all alone and told God that I was all his and that I would give him all the glory. I knew this wouldn't be an easy mountain to climb, but it was my mountain, and I was going to get to the top no matter how long it took. At this point, it was all in God's hands, and I would accept it and learn and grow my relationship with him.

I kept telling myself also that there were people who had to live their whole life needing help all day, every day, and that I should be grateful to still have my leg. It felt so good to let everything out and stop holding it all in. I never liked to express how I felt to others and would keep everything to myself. This didn't change after my accident, but I did have moments where I would talk to God and pray by myself. Even though I had bad days where I just wanted to throw my hands up and quit, I also had great days that made the bad days easier to get through. Everyone's kind words and visits helped a lot as well.

One night, a few days before Valentine's day, I allowed my parents to go out to eat for the first time in a month by themselves under one condition—their curfew was midnight. It was not only Valentine's day in a few days but my parent's anniversary as well. My mom asked Heather Gee to come stay with me that night. Heather had become a second mom to me in the summer of 2012 and stayed by our sides through everything. The night my parents went out, I was so nervous to have someone else take care of me. If I hadn't known Heather so well, I couldn't have done it. My mom and dad were the only two that had taken care of me since the day of my accident. Heather brought dinner, and we watched movies. She did an amazing job taking care of me and kept a smile on my face the whole time.

During that time period, I had to go to the doctors in Dallas every week. It was always hard to be in the car for two hours with my leg having to stay straight across the back seat. When we arrived at Children's Medical Center in Dallas, the whole hospital staff that worked on me during my stay at the hospital would be in the room when the doctors came in.

First, we had to go to one floor and visit my plastic surgeon, Dr. Smartt. He would look at my skin graft and make sure everything was healing the way it should. One spot of my skin graft was having trouble healing, but, over time, it finally healed. I would also get to increase my leg-dangling time each time we went for a visit. As the weeks passed, he would add five minutes to my dangling twice a day. Every time, they took pictures of my leg and thigh where they had taken the skin and also my back where they had taken the entire latissimus dorsi muscle.

I was a teaching case throughout my whole accident because my doctors had never seen a leg injury to that extent. After we visited my plastic surgeon and took pictures, we would head down to my orthopedic surgeon, Dr. Riccio, where I always had to take x-rays. Afterward, we would go into a room and wait for the doctor. When he came into the room, he examined my bone to see if it was healing. Each time, my bone had not started healing because I was not able to walk on my leg to create blood flow down to the broken bone. My orthopedic surgeon was not too worried about it at the time. After all my visits were over, we would get lunch and then head back home. Sometimes we would meet up with Mark and Amber Hapka.

Just like when we were staying in the hospital, routines became an everyday thing for us at home as well. During the week of spring break, we went shopping for my eighth-grade dance dress. I knew I most likely wouldn't be back in school by the time of the dance, but I didn't want to miss it. It was one of the hardest things to try on a formal dress while in a wheelchair trying to keep my leg straight, with tons of bandages on.

After spring break in March, I started my first day of Homebound. I was so nervous because I'd never done anything like this before, and I'd never met my Homebound teacher. My mom worked on her stuff while I sat in the living room working on my classwork. My Homebound teacher, Mrs. Fort, came twice a week for two hours to bring me work that I missed from school, and it was a lot. I was so far behind from being out for three months, but with the help of Mrs. Fort, I was catching back up pretty quickly.

When Mrs. Fort wasn't there, I had to finish the work that I could on my own so she could turn it back in to the school when she came the next time. After a few weeks of my mom being home, it was time for her to go back to work in order to keep our medical insurance going. My BB would come sit with me throughout the days, and I am so thankful for her because she helped me with anything I needed and would sit there while I was doing Homebound school.

In the months following my accident, and after having that breakdown and putting everything in God's hand, I was still trying to find out why this had happened to me. As I thought things through, I realized I should be thankful for the things I had and not dwell so much on what had happened. I had a leg, and, yes, there was still a chance it would be taken from me, but I had my leg for now. I could have been seriously injured in that accident and experienced more than just a leg injury—I could have lost my life.

One day toward the end of March, I told my mom all the conversations I had been having with myself and things that I had been praying to God about. I told her I wanted to be saved. My mom always tried her hardest to remind me how much God loves me and wants the best for me, and she always wondered what it would take for me to be saved. When I told my mom, she was so happy because she realized that, through this accident, I was able to understand the sacrifices God made for me, leading me to ask him into my heart.

On Easter Sunday, April 6, 2013, I went to church and asked God into my life. At the time, I was shy and didn't like to be in front of big crowds, so, lucky for me, it was storming that day, and the church power was out. That made me feel much more comfortable going down the aisle by candlelight. I was, unfortunately, unable to be baptized because my leg could not be submerged in water. My pastor told me that the day would come when we could do the baptism.

I had never felt closer to God than I did in the moment I asked him into my life and to forgive me of my sins. I knew this was just the start in growing my relationship with God, but I knew it was a good start. I also knew this was not going to be easy and that I would be tested at every point in this climb to the top. However, I knew as long as I kept the faith that was still growing inside of me and my trust in God, nothing was going to stop me.

On April 28, I threw a huge birthday party since I was unable to have my birthday party back in January because of the accident. It was a dance party, and even though I was in a wheelchair, I danced the night away with all my friends. I laughed for the first time in a while and smiled the whole night. At that time, I was able to dangle my leg for a whole hour at a time. I waited until the end of the night to dangle my leg so I could walk on crutches for at least an hour during my party.

That night was exactly what I needed to help me get back to a somewhat normal teenage life. I was having to be an adult so much those previous months with making decisions about my leg that it felt so good not to have to think and just dance. Instead of talking medical terms, I was able to talk with my friends about things that were going on at school, just like a normal teenager should.

A few weeks after asking God into my life and my 14th birthday party, I went to my doctor's appointment, and they told me I could start putting a little pressure on my leg with a walking boot. However, I did have to keep my leg up when I wasn't walking on my crutches, once again causing inconvenience.

As the month of April came to an end and May arrived, it was time for my eighth-grade dance. Spending the whole day getting ready was so much fun because it felt good to get all dressed up, take pictures, eat with friends, and dance. Even though I was still on crutches and would get tired quickly from being on my leg, it was nice to sit there just talking and laughing with friends. Again, it just felt good to be a normal teenager instead of talking about medical issues all the time. My cousin Danielle was also by my side the whole night, making sure I was having fun even if I wasn't dancing with everyone.

I did Homebound school for about two months, and about three weeks before school got out, I went back to the doctors and asked my plastic surgeon if it would be okay to go back to school for the last two weeks of the year. He said I had been doing very well with my dangling and that it was okay with him, but he wanted me to leave each class five minutes early to avoid the crowded halls. He also told me that my leg was only to be down while I was walking on crutches from class to class. When I got to where I was going, I had to put my leg up on a chair.

I was so excited to be able to finish out my eighth-grade year, even though it was for two weeks. However, as a typical teenager, I was not excited about waking up early again. The last two weeks of school went by fast, and all my friends and people I'd never met were helpful through it all, making for an easier transition back. My teachers worked well with me throughout the last two weeks.

Once back at school, I had to take the STAAR tests that I had missed while I was out of school. As my eighth-grade year came to an end, I found out that I failed one of my STAAR tests and would have to go to summer school for two weeks. I was devastated because of everything I had been through, and to top it all off, I failed my first STAAR test. I felt like, over time, when something was going well, I would get knocked right back down with some kind of bad news.

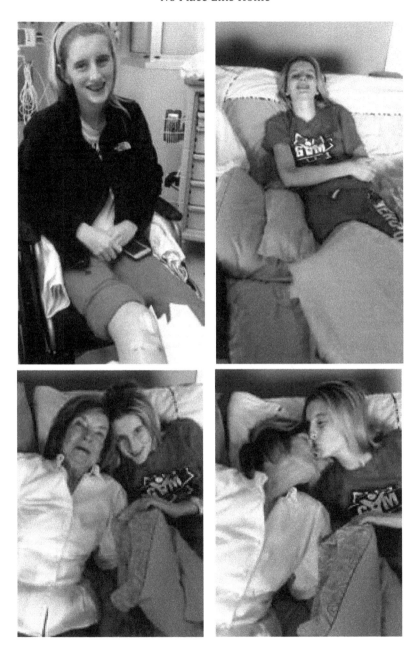

Leaving the hospital and arriving home from the hospital to see my sweet Mimi for the first time in almost a month

The first time holding Zendaya after Mom and Dad brought her home. She was the light in my life at the time and exactly what I needed.

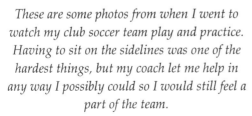

These are some photos from when I went to watch my club soccer team play and practice. Having to sit on the sidelines was one of the hardest things, but my coach let me help in any way I possibly could so I would still feel a part of the team.

Dr. Riccio is the one in the purple shirt, and he was my orthopedic surgeon. Dr. Smartt is the one in blue scrubs, and he was my plastic surgeon.

Sunday, April 6, 2013, Easter Sunday—the day I accepted Jesus into my life and asked him to forgive me of my sins.

My 14ᵗʰ birthday party where we celebrated my birthday three months after the actual day

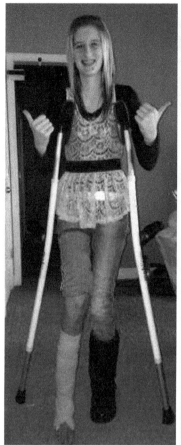
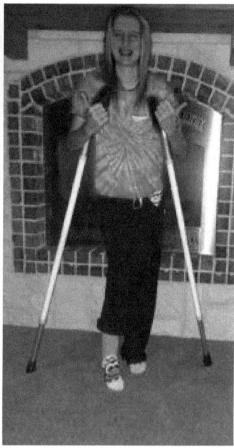

This is what the dangling process consisted of. I would usually try to get up and walk around on crutches while letting my leg down for however long I was allowed to at the time.

The eighth-grade dance. They honored me with a plaque for my courage and determination.

My first day back to school since my accident. Who better to have by my side than my cousin Danielle?

5

A Long Summer with Ups and Downs

THE SUMMER OF 2013 FINALLY STARTED, BUT, FOR me, it was about to be the longest summer ever. I had to start summer school to help prepare me to retake the STAAR test. That lasted for about two weeks. I had to get up every morning and go, and we would usually finish sometime in the afternoon. My grandpa on my mom's side would pick me up every day. I was still on crutches and could only have my leg down when I walked to where I was going, and then I had to put it right back up.

When it was time to take the STAAR test, I was a nervous wreck because I had failed it the first time and had never failed a STAAR test before. I went in there saying, *whatever happens, happens, and as long as I do my best, it will be okay.* I prayed every night that week before my test for God to help me pass. After I finished, it was finally summer for me. I was unable to find out my results until closer to the start of the next school year.

Summer, summer, summer is what every kid looks forward to each year—no school, just swimming, vacations, and hanging with friends, but I had already been out of school for almost five months because of my leg. Now, I'm like any other kid and love when we don't have school, but

I never realized how much I missed it and how much it meant to me until it was taken away from me during that time. Wait just one second—did I just say I missed school?

I was unable to swim that whole summer because of my leg. The skin graft was still healing, so it couldn't be in water other than pouring water over it to clean it. We all hung out at each other's houses, but it was hard having fun at someone's house because I usually had to sit and watch them since my leg was in a boot and on crutches. Also, with my leg not being able to be down a lot at a time, I had to stay seated. It was always hard to sit there and watch them swimming and running around.

We went on some vacations that summer, but it was just to Dallas to watch my soccer team play. I rarely missed a practice or a game as long as I was feeling well enough to go. Even though I couldn't play, I still wanted to be there to support my team. It was hard to sit there and watch something I had done most of my life and not be able to jump into the game and play.

When we went to Dallas on the weekends, Heather, Sophie, and the rest of their family came with us as well. You would think we'd be tired of Dallas after being there so much for doctor visits and soccer, but it was the easiest and closest place to vacation, and there were lots of things in Dallas that I wanted to do in addition to watching soccer.

I missed out on most of the summer due to going back and forth for follow-ups to check the progress of my recovery. However, my parents did try their hardest to make sure I enjoyed summer as much as I could. They always tried to make sure we stayed in Dallas on the weekends and did whatever I could do while being in a boot and on crutches.

Instead of going to doctor visits every week, we started going every other week, still visiting both doctors. Dr. Smartt was proud of how well my skin graft was doing, so he wanted me to start putting pressure on my leg with my boot on as well as with crutches. I was so scared to start putting pressure down because I didn't want to do something that would mess my leg up even more.

Dr. Riccio was also very proud of how far I had come, but he knew I wasn't out of the woods yet because one part of my bone was still not healing. It was always the hardest thing going into a visit and getting notified that my bone was not healing—bad report after bad report. It got to the point where every time, I knew what the doctor was going to say next. He thought that now that I could put pressure on my leg, the compression and blood flow might help the broken part of the bone to heal.

On June 28, 2013, I once again experienced another setback. I went for a follow-up with my orthopedic surgeon, and he told me that even with me being able to put pressure on my leg, my bone was still not healing. He said I needed surgery very soon to help my bone heal. At this point, I was so angry and kept asking, "Why?" Why me? Why did this have to happen to me, a kid who worked hard every day, always willing to help others?

I know I said I was putting everything in God's hands and trying my hardest to find the positive in all the bad that was happening. At this point, I wondered why I even kept trying. I wanted to call it quits. I started questioning God again at this point in my climb to the top of the mountain. I said, "God, give me a sign or reason why you did this to me. I placed everything in your hands and told you to take all the good and bad. I even asked to be saved on Easter Sunday to show you how much this all meant to me. So why am I still getting bad news after bad news?"

We got home from Dallas, and I went straight to bed. I woke up the next morning and realized that everything I was questioning yesterday was wrong. I prayed to God and said, "I understand that there is a reason for all of this and that I just have to trust you. I know I might not find out the reason why for years down the road, but I know you want me to grow closer to you, be strong, and show others who you are, Father. I know I asked to be saved on Easter Sunday, and I know that wasn't enough for you. I know you want every ounce of my heart. It's just so hard sometimes to remember that, Father. I know you want me to be able to show others the work you are doing in my life, but it is so hard to smile and tell everyone everything is going to be okay when I keep getting these outcomes at doctors' appointments."

After talking to God that morning in my room by myself, I walked down to my grandma's house on my crutches and talked to her. My Mimi is someone I can always talk to and count on because even if I was going through a lot of pain, she was going through something ten times worse, with a lot more pain than I had. She ached every day of her life. She had heart problems, and her spine was the shape of the letter S from scoliosis.

Mimi would always tell me that God had a plan for me. I might not have seen it then, but I would eventually. She said she was there with me every step of the way to help me and push me to the finish line. She said that she could not wait to see what was in my future and to see me walk and run on that soccer field again. She reminded me that God was working in all of our lives each and every day. The outcomes might not have always been what we want, but they were what he wanted for us, in his perfect timing. These words of encouragement from someone who meant the absolute world to me were everything that I needed to hear that day.

My mom and the orthopedic surgeon discussed when I should have my next surgery. On July 17, 2013, I went to Dallas for surgery number eight. This surgery was not a big surgery. The surgeons wanted to try to remove the screws from my ankle to give me more motion when I walked, causing more compression, which would hopefully help the bone would heal. When I got to the hospital, I was so nervous. You would think after going into surgery seven times that I would be a pro at this, but no, I was a nervous wreck.

One of my greatest fears throughout this journey was that I would wake up during one of my surgeries. But I had the best surgical team every time I went into surgery, who took the best care of me. After being in surgery for about five hours, my mom got the call that I was done and going into a room. When I woke up, Dr. Riccio came in and gave me an update. They tried to take the screws out, but my ankle was too weak and still needed them for support. Worried that my ankle would crumble, he put new screws in and said I should keep walking on it, and we would see what happened. So once again, just another painful waiting game.

The next day I was able to go home, and this was a relief because I did not want to stay there any longer. My parents spent the rest of my summer making sure I had the most fun in Dallas. We went to concerts, the aquarium, and my soccer games. We probably should have just bought a house in Dallas that summer!

In August, I had my first experience helping someone else. I met an amazing 10-year-old boy from Plano named Jackson Koster who had been involved in a similar ATV accident. I spent about an hour and a half at his house with my parents and his family. It was one of the most heartwarming experiences. Not only was it helpful for Jackson to hear my story, but it was also helpful for me to hear his story and how much it meant for me to come and talk to him.

At that moment, I knew this was one of the reasons this happened to me; I was able to encourage him to keep going even if it gets tough. I enjoyed seeing Jackson's face go from so sad to so relieved that someone else was going through something similar. I knew also that I had found my passion to help inspire as many people as I possibly could and knew I needed to keep going through my journey to show just how amazing God was.

The time I spent with Jackson made my heart burst wide open to let God all the way in because it made me feel so good inside. Everything had pieced itself together as to why this happened to me. I knew that I was not only to tell others not to give up but also to tell them how amazing God's work can be in each of our lives, if we just let him have every ounce of our hearts. He was using me to tell others about him.

I started physical therapy that summer, and I did not like it one bit. It wasn't that the people weren't nice to me; it was just that I always wanted to do more and more. They took the best care of me every time I went. I even thought I might like to practice physical therapy one day. Although I did physical therapy for several months, my bone was still not healing. When we went for my last doctor's visit of the summer, they told us it was time to start thinking of more options to try to save my leg. This worried me because I was thinking of amputation.

My orthopedic surgeon told me I had two surgeries to choose from in order to try to save my leg. He prepared me for the possibility that neither would work and that amputation was most likely the next option. I was freaking out and so scared. He explained that one of the surgeries was called a bone graft from the iliac crest in my hip. It's where they take a piece of my hip bone, iliac crest, and place it where my tibia was not healing. The next option for surgery was what is called an external fixator, known as an ilizarov frame. That is where they put this big metal device on your leg with multiple pins and rods, 13 to be exact, connecting to the bones with these big halo looking rings to hold everything together.

My doctors told me that my best option would be the external fixator. They informed my parents and me there was a chance that if I did the bone graft surgery, the tibia fracture might reject the bone graft from my hip, but I did not want to wear this scary metal device for everyone to see.

They said I didn't have to choose right away because I needed to make sure I was making the right decision. I was so confused as what to do. My heart was set on doing the bone graft, but everyone was trying to talk me out of it. My parents wanted me to do the external fixator as well, but they also wanted to make sure I was happy.

After getting the news that I needed to start thinking about surgery again, I found out I had passed the STAAR test. Also, during the process, I had started my first day of high school—freshman year, the year every kid waits for. You're finally in high school, and the last four years of grade school start. However, most kids look forward to starting high school with sports, band, or other high school activities, but I was unable to participate in any of these, and it was hard for me to try to wrap my head around the idea of having to watch from the sidelines while my friends got to do these things.

I also had to start freshman year on crutches and in a walking boot. I did get to leave classes five minutes early because of this, and my teachers and classmates were all helpful. Also, not only was I starting high school, which was stressful enough, but I had to make a decision soon about what surgery I wanted. My mom tried everything possible to help me pick the right surgery, which was the external fixator, per the surgeons. At this point I wanted to do the bone graft, so we went and got some other opinions just to see what others would say.

High school is an important time—the point when most girls start caring about the way they look. It was hard for me to try to wrap my head around having to wear this big, ugly external fixator on my leg for the first year of my high school life. Also, my leg already had a huge scar on it from the first big surgery where they put the skin graft on. Everyone we talked to said that the external fixator was most likely my best option, but I still wanted the bone graft. All I could think about was all these people were telling me what's best for me, but none of them had had an external fixator before to explain what it was like.

One day during September, my mom was on Facebook late at night scrolling through her newsfeed. She came across a picture with a girl who had an external fixator on her leg and started reading about her. She was in the Boston Marathon bombing and had leg injuries similar to mine. My mom searched for her on Facebook and messaged her that same night asking if she could reach out to me with some encouragement to do the fixator. My mom explained my injury and journey for the past nine months. My mom knew that it was farfetched and never thought that she would message back because this person was a complete stranger to us. I never knew my mom had messaged her.

On Halloween, October 31, 2013, my mom was up working late, the girl responded, and they talked on the phone for hours that night until 5 a.m. When my mom came home from work, she said, "Hey, you're probably going to get a friend request from this person on Facebook." I looked at her like she was crazy, and she started telling me everything. This is how we came to know Rebekah Gregory, now Rebekah Varney.

Summer 2013 vacations to a concert and to the aquarium in Dallas

Family picture before my eighth surgery during the summer of 2013.

Jackson Koster, the boy I met to give some encouraging words to help him get through his journey

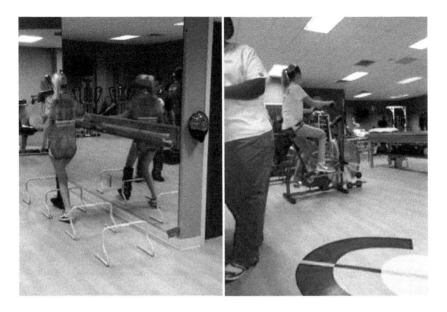

Physical therapy during the summer to try to get my bone to start healing

Of course, my summer also consisted of watching my soccer team practices and games.

My first day of freshman year of high school

6

Someone Who Gets It

I ACCEPTED REBEKAH GREGORY VARNEY'S FRIEND request on Facebook, and we started getting to know each other. Over a few weeks, she filled me in on all the details of having an external fixator placed on an extremity. She was completely honest. I loved this about her because she had personal experience wearing one. It was so nice hearing about this device from someone who knows what it is like, rather than hearing it from the surgeons or watching videos about them. That November, I finally decided to pick the external fixator. Over the next two months, I had appointments to start planning for my next surgery.

It was a lot for a 14-year-old to handle and to take it all in. Knowing that I was about to have this huge metal device on my leg scared me. It was so nice to have Rebekah there to comfort me even if it was only through the phone. The surgeons planned my surgery for January 21, 2014, a day after my one-year anniversary of the wreck.

Before my surgery, we decided to celebrate my 15th birthday early because we did not know how long I would be in the hospital afterward. I invited a few friends to come eat on the Friday before my surgery. Little did I know I was going to have the surprise of a lifetime and a special visitor. The Monday before the dinner, my mom asked me what classes I had on Friday, and I didn't think anything of it at the time. She also asked if I had anything planned Thursday night, and I said no.

I asked her why, and she said, "Your dad and I wanted to take you to eat for a family birthday before your party on Friday night."

On Wednesday, my mom asked if it would be okay for me to miss school on Friday. I told her that I needed to go to school.

She said, "Okay it's just we are going to be getting home late Thursday night."

I said, "Why? Where are we going?"

She said, "We are going to Dallas to eat dinner."

I thought to myself how weird that was, especially on a school night. I told my mom okay, but at the same time, I thought something was up.

I kept thinking about going to Dallas on a school night and why she would want me to miss school on Friday. Then it all clicked. I thought, *we are going to pick Rebekah up from the airport*. I kept asking my mom, but she kept saying, "I don't know." Thursday after school, we headed to Dallas. I fell asleep in the backseat on the way there, but when we got to the airport, I woke up. I noticed that we were parked, and I could hear my parents talking about where she would come out. I pretended to still be asleep as I listened to them talk. I knew Rebekah was coming to visit. I leaned up and said, "Mom, I told you we were picking up Rebekah."

We pulled up to the front of the airport, and there she was. She was still in a walking boot and on crutches also, with the assistance of a wheelchair. I will never forget that day. Rebekah was going to stay the whole weekend with me before my surgery. On the car ride back, we talked the whole time, and even when we got home that night, we stayed up until 1 a.m. talking. The next day I went to school, and my mom and Rebekah hung out around town.

That night we went to my birthday dinner, and I had an amazing time with friends and family. That Saturday, we spent the whole day lying around the house, and Rebekah told us all about her journey. Rebekah and I laughed because we wore the same size shoes and the leg that she wore a boot on at the time was the opposite of my leg. I told her that every time we get a new pair of boots, I would send her the right one and she said she would send me the left one. We continued that Saturday getting to know each other and laughing for hours about different things.

Hearing all about her journey helped me in so many ways. She was a beautiful person not only on the outside but on the inside. She had endured hard times throughout her journey, yet she still managed to wake up every day and find the good out of life with a smile on her face. It made me realize just how beautiful life in itself is. She had every reason to give up and quit and to hate the world because her injuries were intentionally inflicted, but, no, she decided to stand tall, facing her obstacles, traveling the world, and sharing her testimony with others.

She taught me so much that weekend about life in general. She became like family, the sister I never had but often longed for. It's so crazy to think someone I had only known for three days could make this kind of impact on my life. The hardest of all goodbyes was when we dropped her off at the airport in Dallas that Sunday. I hugged her goodbye, and we told each other we would see each other very soon. She said she wished she could be here the day of my surgery and that she would be thinking about and praying for me.

Someone came to help her and push the wheelchair so she could board her flight. I just remember crying and thinking about how those three days with her impacted my life for the good. Before she left, she said, "One thing is for sure. The day you step back on that soccer field for the first time, I will be there in the stands cheering you on."

We continue to stay in touch with Rebekah to this day and see her as much as we can. She lives almost four hours away, so it's hard to have the distance between us, but we try to see each other every chance we get. Every day, she manages to teach me something new about life. She has had to deal with so much throughout her life, but, somehow, she still manages to be so close to God, keeping a smile on her face and never losing faith in what she believes.

I know there are hard days for her because there were hard days for me as well. She's also had a lot of good throughout her journey and continues every day to tell people the importance of not giving up. She always told me that if at any point I ever felt like giving up, she would kick my butt. She said that she would always be here for me, and if I ever needed her, she was just a phone call away.

Rebekah was literally an angel that God sent me. Without her, I would not be where I am today. She not only pushed me to not give up, but she also taught me the importance of my experiences. She has taught me to inspire other people just like she did. She has and still does make such an impact on my life, and I want to pay it forward by doing the same for someone else.

Without her telling me all about the external fixator, I probably would have gone with the other surgery, a bone graft from my hip, which would have been way more extensive with no guarantee it would heal my bone. If this surgery had failed, I would have either had to have the external fixator or start thinking about amputation. I can only hope to be half the woman she is when I am older. I will forever be grateful and thankful to have Rebekah in my life.

This picture was taken moments after we picked Rebekah up from the airport, the very first time I met her.

My pre-15th-birthday dinner celebration with Rebekah

*Some more pre-celebration birthday
dinner pictures*

Saying goodbye after an amazing weekend of celebrating, visiting, and getting me prepared for surgery. Moments after this picture, I was in tears from saying goodbye.

7

In God's Timing

CHRISTMAS BREAK HAD COME TO AN END, AND IT was time for the spring semester of my freshman year to start. I went to school in a walking boot and on one crutch. I only went to school for two weeks because I was about to have my external fixator put on. When I agreed to go with the external fixator, I told my doctors that the only way I would do it is if they let me do Homebound school again like I did when I first got hurt. I didn't want to have to wear this big metal device around my leg walking up and down the hallways at school, fearing that kids would bump into me. I also knew it would be a huge adjustment, so I knew it was best, mentally and physically, if I did Homebound.

During those two weeks at school, I was to be switched into the soccer class at school so I could still feel a part of the team. I got to be the manager and go to all the games. I filmed games and also helped with practices. Although it was very hard to have to sit and watch my friends play high school soccer their first year of high school, something I have dreamed about my whole life, I was just glad to be included and feel a part of the team. The older girls on the team were all nice and made me feel right at home.

The day before my ninth surgery, we went to the hospital to go over everything, along with my pre-op. Oh, did I mention I had to switch hospitals? I was in love with Dallas Children's Hospital and finally had gotten used to the nurses and all my doctor visits being there, but since I had chosen the external fixator, I had to go to The Scottish Rite Hospital, which wasn't far from the other hospital. The other hospital didn't have the proper equipment to do the surgery. My orthopedic surgeon at Dallas Children's Hospital had privileges at both hospitals, so he was able to be there. I also had to have a new orthopedic surgeon, named Dr. Wimberley, who would work with my other one because he would be doing the surgery. The Scottish Rite Hospital specializes in the external fixator.

I was so nervous about having surgery at a different hospital because I had never been there. The day before, we met with everyone who would be in the OR with me for my surgery. Everyone was nice and could tell I was extremely nervous about it. They all kept telling me I was in good hands and that everything would be okay.

While we were there, I met the nurse who would be on my case while I had the external fixator on. Her name was Johanna Pool, and she was the most amazing nurse they could have put on my case. She was so nice and knew I was nervous about what was ahead and tried to make me feel happy. I am so thankful to have had her on my case because she made everything better and is now a close friend.

While at the hospital, my friend Sophie and her mom surprised me. When I came around the corner, they were both sitting there waiting for me. It was so good to have them there because they helped keep me laughing and as calm as I could be while my parents had to handle all the paperwork. They spent the rest of the afternoon going with me in and out of different appointments I had throughout the hospital.

Once we finished with that, we were able to leave. We all went to eat at Dave and Buster's and played some games before the big day. I ate as much as I could before it was time to, once again, not eat anymore after midnight. It was then time to head back to the hotel. We said goodbye to Sophie and Heather and left the restaurant. I said my prayers to God that night and went right to sleep, so nervous about what lay ahead these next few months.

Morning came very early that day for me, and we went straight to the hospital. I was so scared and nervous, more than ever before. They took me up to my room. I got undressed, put my hospital gown on, and waited for them to get me for surgery. While waiting, my mom wanted to take our family picture as we did before all my surgeries. We said our family prayers, and it was time for me to go back to surgery. It lasted a few hours, and everything went well.

They had broken my tibula in a new spot at the top of my shin, which is what they had to do for this surgery. The surgeons were now able to push the tibia down into the other broken area that wasn't healing, so it would hopefully be able to heal with time. The gap where they broke the top of my tibia is where the new healing process would begin. Once back in my room, I was in lots of pain and not ready to see this device on my leg. At least it was under bandages for now.

The night finally came after a long day of surgery. Because the rooms weren't big enough to sleep two people, my dad couldn't stay with my mom and I as he had at Children's, so he stayed at Ronald McDonald House, which is where families from out of town could stay to help with expenses when they had a child at the hospital. I didn't like the idea of my dad not being able to stay in the room with me and my mom.

The next day when I woke up and tried to eat breakfast, I was unable to because my throat was burning so bad. Anytime I swallowed, my throat would hurt. During surgery, they used too big of a tube when they put me under, and when they took it out after surgery, it scratched my throat. I knew it wasn't their fault because it was my first surgery at this hospital, and they didn't have on file what size tube was used in prior surgeries. I was only able to eat very little amounts at a time and unable to drink anything except for Gatorade because everything else burned when it went down my throat.

As the days passed, we got a system down. Every morning, my mom would help get me cleaned up, and then my dad would come with breakfast. My mom would then go to where my dad was staying, take a shower, and get cleaned up while my dad stayed with me at the hospital. While my mom was gone, my dad and I would go down and do my therapy with the physical therapist at the hospital.

We started therapy in small increments by just doing simple things like learning how to bend my knee with the fixator on. I also had to turn these dice looking things on the fixator four times daily, which would eventually stretch my leg to get some length back that I had lost. This process would allow bone growth where they had broken it, allowing healing. They also took the rod and screws out when they put the external fixator on. It wasn't that painful at first, but as time went on, having to turn them got harder each day and started to hurt.

A few days after the surgery, I was still feeling sick to my stomach and would have hot flashes. My face was also very itchy. We couldn't figure out what was causing me so much trouble this time post-surgery. At first, we thought maybe it was from the anesthesia. One night my nurse came in to put medicine in my IV pump, and my mom asked what they were giving me. When the nurse told my mom the names of the medications, she was concerned that I might be having an allergic reaction. My mom asked if the nurse could print off the side effects of those medicines. When the nurse brought the papers into my room, she realized I was allergic to both of those medicines. We told my doctors, and they discontinued them and put me on something else. I finally started to feel so much better after they took me off those medicines.

After being in the hospital for a week, therapy started getting harder. It was time for me to walk on my leg. Not only was this the first time to walk without the boot on for support, but I also had this huge device on that didn't help me feel any better about walking for the first time. The therapist told me to stand up and put weight on my leg to begin. After a few minutes of getting used to just standing on it with weight, I had to start walking. I cried a lot when I was walking. I was in pain, but a lot of the tears were because I was just scared that it was going to snap again.

After that one therapy session, walking started getting easier. I would even try to challenge myself with walking down the hallway using a walker—with my dad right behind me, of course. One day, I even tried to walk all the way to the therapy room. I almost made it. I got a little more than halfway and got tired and started to feel sick. Everything started to get as easy as it could. I had lots of visitors come and visit me. I even got to see Mark and Amber again. Jackson and his mom came up to visit as well.

That second week in the hospital was my birthday week. Yep, that's right. I was going to have to spend not one birthday in the hospital but two birthdays. I know there are a lot of kids out there who have had to spend way more birthdays than I did in the hospital. Trust me—I have so much more respect for those kids now. At least for this birthday, I would be awake, unlike my 14th birthday when I was in an operating room for 12 hours.

On the day of my 15th birthday, I woke up and went to therapy early so I could have the rest of the day. My mom had gone back into Longview to take care of something, so it was just my dad and me for the day. We watched TV and relaxed in the room. I received so many phone calls and text messages that day. The evening finally came around, and my mom had called us and told us to meet her in the hospital cafeteria. My dad helped me get back into my wheelchair, and we headed down the hall. When we went around the corner, there was a waiting area. I looked over at it and then looked away, but I quickly realized I had seen someone I knew over there, so I told my dad to go back.

My mom and Heather, Sophie, two of my other friends, Jackson's mom, Jackson's little brother, and Jackson were all sitting in the waiting area with balloons, presents, and a cake. I smiled and even teared up a little. We visited for a couple of hours, took pictures, ate cake, and I opened my gifts. I was so thankful that they took time out of their day to come see me at the hospital on my birthday. Overall, it was a pretty good birthday for being stuck at the hospital.

A couple of more days went by, and it was time to leave. They showed us how to clean my leg and the pins and rods, all 13 of them, that went into my leg every morning and night. They told me if I needed anything, they were just a phone call away. Before heading back home to Longview, we went to a US Women's National soccer game in Frisco. My friend Sophie and her parents met us there as well.

We got these tickets in December as a Christmas gift and an early birthday gift for me. At the time, we had seats a little closer to the bottom, but since I was in a wheelchair, my mom had to call and get me in wheelchair accessible seating. I didn't care where I had to watch the game from as long as I could be there to watch them. I can't tell you how much I am a huge fan of the US Women's National Team. I often dreamed of being a part of that team. That's what I wanted to be when I was older. I loved every second of that night. It made me smile and forget about being in a wheelchair or that I had this device on my leg.

After the game, we headed back to the Ronald McDonald House, where we stayed one more night before heading home. That night, one of my favorite nurses from Children's, Amber Hunter, came to see me and visit for a while. Morning came, and it was time to head home and get adjusted to life at home with this fixator on. The trip home wasn't too bad this time because we were pretty used to it.

The very next Tuesday, I surprised my high school soccer girls by coming to watch them play. I rolled up in my wheelchair, and they were all smiles. I sat on the sidelines with them and watched. It was cold that night, so the girls who were playing all gave me their big jackets to lay on me. After that game, I tried to make as many more games as I could.

Cleaning my leg became routine for us, and I never had a hard time picking out outfits for wherever we were going—sweatpants and a t-shirt it was. I was only able to put sweatpants on over my external fixator, and t-shirts were the only thing that went with it. For a while, I slept on the couch again until I was used to having the device on while I slept. I eventually started sleeping my bed again.

Homebound school had started up again, and I was able to get the same Homebound teacher, Mrs. Fort. She was awesome and always so helpful. Freshman year was a lot harder than eighth grade. I always got lost while doing biology and algebra. My mom had reached out to both of my teachers for those two classes to see if they could help me. My biology teacher, Mrs. Howard, and my algebra teacher, Mr. Kelley, were both willing to help me. They scheduled times to come to my house and explain to me and my mom how to do the worksheets so my mom could help me when they weren't there. I will never be able to tell them how thankful I am for both of them. Without them coming to help me and my Homebound teacher, Mrs. Fort, I probably wouldn't have passed my freshman year of high school.

I had doctors' visits and x-rays every two weeks or so. Guess what? Every time we went before, my bone was not healing, but this time it was finally healing. Finally, for the first time in a year and half, we had good news! I knew I was on the road to being back on that soccer field. I could finally see a light at the end of the very long tunnel. The doctors told me they wanted me to start using crutches to walk around instead of the wheelchair. They also wanted me to start walking without crutches any chance I got. This made me very nervous because although the blood flow was fine, and we had finished the dangling process, I was still scared that I was going to mess my bone up and have to start all over.

The end of the school year was just around the corner, and I was still on Homebound getting used to walking with crutches. When I was around the house, I wouldn't use crutches. With the school year close to ending, it was time to take the STAAR test again. I was freaking out about these tests because if you don't pass, you don't go to the next grade, and I was on Homebound for a whole semester. This meant that even though I was still able to do my schoolwork, I was unable to be in a classroom, learning the topics with specialized teachers for each subject. This made me nervous that I wasn't prepared enough for these tests.

A lady from the school came out to my house to sit with me while I took them. It was just like taking them at school, except I was on my couch with my leg propped up. I had the same amount of time as the other students at school. I had to take three tests within three days. During the next month or so, I got the news that I had passed all three of them. That also meant that summer 2014 was right around the corner, but I still had the external fixator on my leg. I knew I would have another long summer ahead of me.

*Day of Pre-Op for the ninth surgery to get the external fixator on.
Sophie came to surprise me and make sure I had a good day, even if
it was spent mostly in the hospital getting ready for surgery the
next day.*

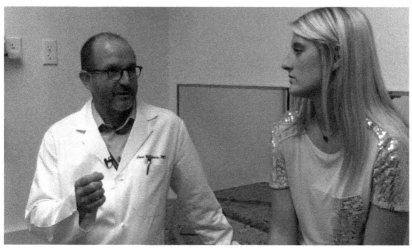

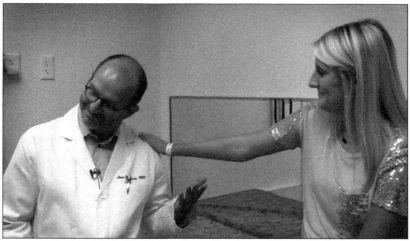

My orthopedic surgeon from Scottish Rite, Dr. Wimberley. I was nervous at first about getting a new surgeon, but I couldn't have asked for a better one to be added to what I like to call my team.

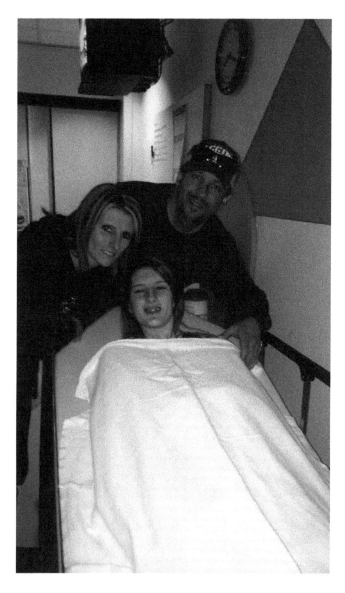

Family picture before the ninth surgery to get the external fixator on.

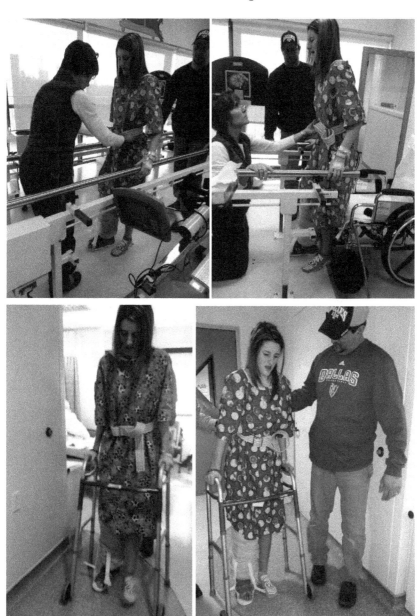

Physical therapy after getting the external fixator on. As you can see by the look on my face, it was very painful to try to walk on my leg for the first time.

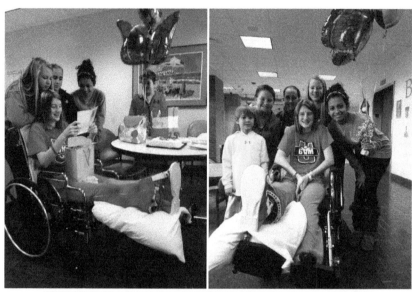

My surprise 15th birthday party thrown in the lobby on my floor in the hospital on my actual birthday.

Attending the US Women's National Team soccer game after
getting out of the hospital

My nurse Amber Hunter from Children's coming to visit me and dropping off a matching bracelet like she had on before I headed back home the next day

Getting home from two weeks in the hospital to snuggle on my sweet little fur babies, Zendaya and Bella

Going to watch my high school soccer team play the next night after getting home from being in the hospital for two weeks. It didn't matter how cold it was; I wanted to be there to support.

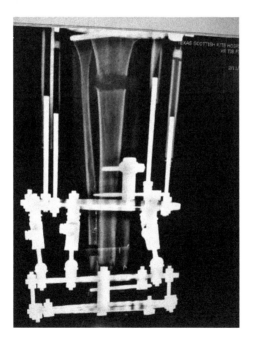

The first x-ray I took that showed a bit of bone healing. You can barely see it, but this was the best news I had heard in a long time.

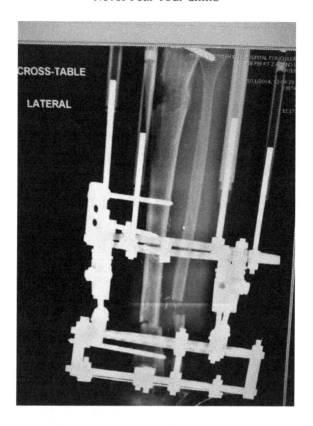

Over the next few months, at every doctor's appointment I went to,
the x-rays kept showing more and more bone growth.

8

My Person

EVERYONE HAS THAT ONE PERSON IN THEIR LIFE who means the absolute world to them and who you would do anything in the world for. For me, that someone was my grandma Mimi. My Mimi means the whole world to me, and I would have done anything in the world for her. Unfortunately, during the time I had the fixator on my leg, she passed away on Saturday, March 29, 2014, around 4:30 in the afternoon.

Losing my Mimi was one of the hardest things I had ever had to go through in my life so far. She was my best friend, and I loved her more than anything. Growing up, I always watched her every move. She would always watch me during the day while my parents were working, so we became very close. She did everything for me, and I couldn't be more thankful for her or her unconditional love.

When we moved to our new home, we moved my Mimi and Papa onto the land with us because Mimi was very sick. She was always in pain but never complained a day in her life about it, or let it show to anyone. Since she lived behind us, I helped her and spent time with her when I wasn't busy.

My Mimi and Papa loved me so very much and always made sure I knew that they did. Papa would pick me up from school because Mimi was too sick to come, and he would have a snack waiting for me in the car that Mimi had sent with him. When I got home from school, Mimi would always have a meal for me. I am forever thankful for that.

My Mimi had always been in and out of the hospital since I could remember. Not only was she in and out of the hospital, but she had also lost one of her sons in 2008, my Uncle Rex. She was one of the most kind-hearted people and was never rude to anyone. Since I was nine at the time my Uncle Rex died, it was hard for me to understand how God could put someone as sweet as her through all this and how he could take such a beautiful soul like my Uncle Rex from this world and allow her to suffer so much mentally and physically.

Anytime I would start to think about that, Mimi would talk to me about it and say, "God always has a path for everyone, and this is just my path. Overcoming it is what God wants me to do, and it was just Rex's time to go home to heaven." I still never could comprehend those words until my accident happened. When I started questioning things again after my accident, she explained that this was my path and that God had a plan for me. I needed to push through it and grow closer to God. Well, that's exactly what I did.

When I first got hurt, one of the hardest things for me was being away from my Mimi. Since she was always in pain, it was hard for her to travel far, so she was unable to come see me the entire time I was in the hospital. That was the longest time I ever had to go without seeing her. After being in the hospital for a month in Dallas, when I came home, she and Papa were the first people I wanted to see. As soon as we pulled into the driveway, Mimi was inside waiting on me. I was so very happy to see her and give her the biggest hug and kiss ever.

The next few months after my accident, anytime I was in pain or felt like giving up, I would think of my Mimi and how she lived in pain 24/7. Anytime I started to complain about having to go to doctors' appointments, I would think of my Mimi and how she had to go to a doctor almost every day. Having her by my side through my accident was everything to me. She would always have just the right thing to say to me when I needed it the most.

In January, when I was having my ninth surgery to get the external fixator on, I had to go without seeing her again for two weeks. During this time, she became very sick and was in more pain than ever. When I got back home, she still was not doing any better, so my mom decided it would be best to take her to the hospital. She spent a few days there and got a little better but not a lot.

A few days went by, and I thought things were starting to get better. One day, I was sitting at home with my Homebound teacher working on schoolwork for her to take back to school for me. My other grandma, BB, was there also and my mom was at work. I noticed my mom pulling down the driveway fast going to my grandparents' house, which was right behind ours. I got my BB to call my mom and see what was going on. I finished up my schoolwork and went straight down to my grandma's house. My mom was getting ready to take her back to the hospital because she was not doing well again.

Let me brag about my mom for a minute because not only did she have to take care of me, but she was also always back and forth from the hospital to home and was working too. She is a real-life superhero in my eyes. My mom was looking at all the options for what would be best for my Mimi. We looked into nursing homes and rehabs that were close to us to see which would be the best fit. When Mimi left the hospital, my mom went with her to the nursing home, but when they got there, my mom suddenly decided she did not want my Mimi in there and would resign from her nursing position at the cardiology clinic.

My mom decided the nursing home was not the best fit for our family and decided to bring my Mimi home where we all helped take care of her. That day when my mom suddenly came home from work, I walked down to my grandparents' house to see what was going on. Mimi was using her oxygen tank and had a sad look on her face. My mom and grandpa were in the living room as well and told me that they had placed Mimi on hospice. My Mimi told me to sit down. She told me that her body was tired and in so much pain that she could not handle it anymore. Tears rolled down my face, and all I kept telling her was that she need to keep fighting like she had always taught me.

After a few minutes, I realized that my Mimi was so tired of fighting and that she was ready to be with her son and God in heaven. As hard as it was for me to say these words to her, I told her it was okay, that she could go and be pain free. When I told her that, she was relieved because all she had ever wanted to do was make me happy. Hearing those words from me told her I understood why she was tired of fighting.

As the day went on, my mom called the rest of the family and told them that Mimi had decided to be placed on hospice care, and we were going to honor her wishes. Everyone started coming over. The next day, reality started to set in, and hospice came and explained everything to us. Family kept coming and going, and I made sure that I was always down there during the day.

I felt like I could not catch a break on this path God had me traveling. Every time I felt like I could see one view from the mountain top, another mountain would pop up in the distance for me to have to overcome.

A few weeks went by, and my Mimi's health was starting to become worse. I knew it would be any day now, so I made sure I was always right by her side. She was still able to talk to us at first, and she made sure all the family was around. She said, "I want you all to make sure you continue to love one another and stay strong as a family."

About three or four days before she passed, she had gotten somewhat better, which is usually called a rally before someone passes. She wanted me to make her coffee, and she wanted to sit up in the chair. I had great hopes and thought this was weird that she was suddenly doing so good. I thought maybe this wasn't her time to go, but the next day, she went downhill again. The hospice nurse told us she only had about two more days with us. I asked the hospice nurse how she could have been doing so well yesterday and downhill the next. She told me it was because everyone usually has a burst of energy before they pass.

Little did we know she was right about those two days. All the family came over because it was a Saturday, and we ordered pizza. We were all sitting around laughing and talking about good memories from the past. I was outside on the porch with my cousins when my Mimi took her last breath in my mom's arms, and my uncle Ricky, who was inside with my mom and Mimi, came outside and told us she was gone. My heart literally stopped, and all I could think about was how was I going to live without seeing my Mimi's sweet face and hearing her voice every day.

The night after she passed, I went outside and just screamed to God. I asked him why he would put someone like me, so young, through all of this. Not only was I going through a serious leg injury that still had not healed, but now he had taken my grandma. I questioned my faith more than I ever have during this time in my life. I could not wrap my head around it at the time. I felt like just giving up and being done. My Mimi wasn't going to be here to see me walk or play soccer. She wasn't going to see me graduate high school and college. She wasn't going to see me get married and would never see me become a mother. But most of all, she wouldn't be here every day of my life. I went to bed that night with all of this on my mind, so you can only imagine how much sleep I got.

We had her visitation that following Monday, and her funeral was on that following Wednesday, April 1, 2014, which would have been her 75th birthday. After all that, my mind was still racing with all those thoughts in my head, and I could not stop thinking about them.

One day my other grandparents came down to visit with me and hang out for the day while my mom ran errands and my dad worked. I remember talking to my BB about how I felt and how it felt so weird not to have my Mimi here. One thing I loved about both sets of my grandparents is they love each other so very much and only wanted the best for their children and grandchildren. My BB told me, "Even though you cannot see her or hear her, she is still here. She is going to watch you continue to grow up and watch you walk again and be right by your side every step of the way, and so am I."

Hearing those words come from my BB meant the absolute world to me because I needed them at that moment. I then realized she did exactly what my Mimi used to do by saying the right thing at the right time. My BB and Papaw mean the absolute world to me, and I could not have gotten past those few weeks without them right there by my side.

A few weeks went by, and it was still not easy for all of us, but it was especially hard for my Papa. My Mimi and Papa were married for 59 years before she passed. They had spent every day of their lives together since they met, and when I say every day, I mean every day. My Papa was so lost without her and didn't know what to do. I made sure he knew he was not alone, that I was here for him, and that we would get through this all as a family.

Betty Joe Taylor, my beautiful, kindhearted, and loving grandmother who was the best Mimi I could have asked for

The bond between my Mimi and me is something that could never be broken. She was the strongest person I have ever known and will probably ever know.

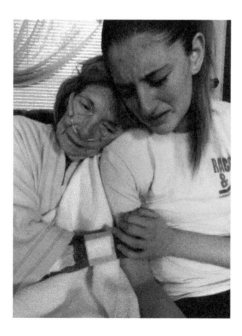

The day she told us that she was so tired of fighting and was ready to go home to heaven.

My Mimi and Papa showed me every day what true love meant. Love one another, and never give up on one another, even if at times it gets hard.

9

Life's a Climb

IN ORDER TO FIGURE OUT WHAT SHE WANTED TO do next, my mom decided to take the rest of the summer off with me, a much-needed emotional break. I knew I had another long summer ahead of me, but little did I know the first week of June, I would have a doctor's appointment that would make my whole summer.

I had no idea what was in store for me as I walked into the hospital. I did my normal routine of checking in, setting my own self up for x-rays because I had become a pro at them, and then waiting on the doctor. Once I got into the room, my parents and I were sitting there talking when Dr. Wimberley and the rest of the team, which I liked to call family, walked into the room.

The first thing Dr. Wimberley asked me was, "Have you eaten anything today?"

"Yes," I said, "I had French fries on the way here, about thirty minutes ago."

He said, "Well, I was about to tell you to go get ready for surgery if you hadn't eaten anything."

My parents and I were so confused. Dr. Wimberley started explaining that my bone was healing and that it was time to get this thing off my leg. We went into the other room to look at x-rays and saw a bone that was healing. It was a feeling I can't explain, and I could not stop smiling.

I asked Dr. Wimberley what we were going to do, and he said, "I want you to come back next week and have surgery to remove the external fixator." I was so extremely happy and overwhelmed with emotions because I knew once this surgery was over, I was finally one step closer to the road of recovery.

The time from the day of that appointment to the surgery date was one of the longest weeks of my life. I felt like it was never going to come. During that week, my mom took me shopping to get some new pants that were not sweatpants. I never thought I could be so tired of sweatpants and ready to put some jeans on.

The day finally came to have my 10th surgery to remove the external fixator from my leg, and by now, you would think I would be a pro at going into surgery, but I was so nervous this time. Once the surgery was over, I stayed in the hospital for a couple of days to make sure everything was okay. It was so weird to get used to my leg being so light and not heavy anymore from the external fixator. When I left the hospital, I went home in a walking boot, just to be safe, and on crutches. The doctors said they wanted me to come back for an appointment in a week, and we went on our way.

During that week, I was getting used to not having this heavy thing on my leg anymore and being back in a walking boot. Also, during that week, I tried not to think about the next appointment where they would probably make me walk without anything on and with no crutches. I was so scared to even think about that because I hadn't walked on my leg in two years without a boot, crutches, or having the external fixator on.

The appointment came, and I did the normal routine again and waited on the doctors. This time it was both Dr. Wimberley and Dr. Riccio. They walked in and asked how everything was and if I was ready to walk. The question I had been waiting for since the day of my accident was also the question I was so scared to be asked. I looked at them with this scared look on my face and was not ready at all. They said everything would be okay.

I asked, "What if my leg snaps and breaks again from putting too much pressure on it?"

They said, "Let's just start with baby steps."

I got out of the chair, took my boot off, and started to put a little pressure on my leg. I stepped a little forward, trying to put a little more pressure on my leg each time. I didn't get to full pressure that appointment, but they told me they didn't want me in the walking boot anymore and to start putting a regular shoe on. As summer went along, I started to put full pressure on my leg but still had a limp every time I walked.

My doctor also told me after we went back for another appointment that it was okay to start getting into the water again. I cannot express to anyone how excited I was to hear those words come out of my doctor's mouth. I had had my leg in shower water and rinsed off but was never allowed to submerge my whole leg in water since the day of my accident. After getting that news, can anyone guess where we went? If you guessed the beach, then you are right. We packed and went straight to the beach, one of my favorite places, for a few days, and it was a much-needed trip.

It was so nice not to worry about a thing and have no doctor appointments for a while. On the way back home, we stopped in Houston, and guess who I got to see? Rebekah and her son Noah. I was so excited to catch up with her because she hadn't seen me since I got the external fixator off. After getting home from the trip, it felt like the rest of summer went by so fast.

The first day of school finally came, and it was my sophomore year of high school. I was so scared because I would be at school without a boot and no crutches. I was scared my leg was going to get tired walking around all day without any type of assistance, which I had been used to for almost two years. Everyone at school was excited to see me up and walking again. All the teachers were nice and helped me if I needed anything.

I was still not released to run or play sports, but I was able to be in the soccer classes as one of their managers and help out. We had a new soccer coach that year named Erickson. He was so understanding about my accident and said he wanted me to still come to all the practices and watch so once I started playing again, I would be on the same page as everyone.

One day during that fall, I came home after school and thought I would put on soccer cleats. Although I was unable to go out and play soccer, it felt so good just to have them on my feet for the first time in almost two years. Also, that fall, I rode my bike for the first time in two years. It felt so good doing these things—things that most people take for granted but I hadn't been able to do in so long.

And then one of the most amazing things happened—I was baptized. I had asked Jesus into my life a little over a year ago but was unable to be submerged in water. The time had finally come. I was so excited and could not wait. On October 19, 2014, we went to church, and my mom and I shared my testimony of how my accident had brought me closer to God. After that, I went with my pastor and was baptized. The feeling of coming out of that water is something I will never be able to put into words. It was like knowing that everything that had happened to me over the last year and a half was meant for this moment. I knew this was still only the beginning of my future with Jesus Christ.

I went for another doctor's appointment that fall and had a big question to ask my doctors. When they walked in, the first thing I asked them was if I could get my permit to drive. Every 15-year-old I knew had their permit, and I had been unable to because of my leg. My doctor examined my leg and checked my ankle movement. I was unable to move my foot up and down still, which is the motion needed to press the brake and gas pedal to drive. The doctor said since I couldn't push my foot down that well, it probably wasn't the best idea to get my permit just yet.

I was extremely sad because that is a milestone every teenager looks forward to in life. Once you get your permit, you're one step closer to getting your driver's license. Dr. Wimberley said if I could come back with my movement better in a week, then he would allow it. He gave me some tips to help. I went home, and every chance I got, I was practicing. I was so determined to improve my ankle movement so he would give me the okay.

I went back that following week, and I was ready to show Dr. Wimberley how much I had improved my movement. He examined my ankle movement and was amazed at how much better it was in just a week. He said, "I think it will be okay for you to get your permit, but I still want you to keep working on the movement."

That following week, my mom took me to take my permit test, and when I got to the eye exam, I was unable to read the letters. The lady said I couldn't get my permit until I got my eyes checked. I walked out of there so mad because I felt like, once again, I was finally getting to the top of my mountain and then getting knocked back down. I know it's not that big of a deal, but I just wished something would go right for once without having to go through anything else or always having obstacles or—as I like to call them—mountains in the way. I went to the eye doctor and had to get glasses because I could not see far away. Then I went back and took my permit test. I passed and was so excited to be able to drive on the open road, but I still had to have a parent in the car with me. I was one step closer to getting my driver's licenses.

The holidays were hard because it was the first year without my grandma. My grandma was always the light of the holidays, and we always hosted the holiday dinners at her and my grandpa's house. I knew my grandma was there with us watching over us and making sure we made it through the holidays.

After Christmas, I had a doctor's appointment on December 30, 2014. I was finally released to run and play soccer again. I couldn't even wrap my head around that. I was on top of the mountain and could finally see the view from the other side. Dr. Wimberley said he wanted me to go easy at first and work my way up. I was so nervous that I told my parents I wanted to get used to playing again on my own. I started working out at home, along with kicking the ball around.

It felt so weird to run again, like I was a small child learning to run for the first time. On January 8, 2015, I went to my club soccer practice and played with them. I took it easy and was so nervous that my leg was going to break again, and I would have to start all over. It was nice to be back out there, even if I wasn't where I used to be as a player. After that practice, I decided to wait again to go back because I was so nervous.

My 16th birthday finally arrived, and I was so excited to finally be 16. However, I was unable to get my license right away because it hadn't been six months since I had gotten my permit. I felt like everything was going well—just another small bump popped up in my path to the top of my mountain view, teaching me once again to be patient, that it was all in God's timing.

I had a birthday party, and it was so much fun not to think about being nervous, getting back on the field, or being sad from not being able to get my driver's license. I got to just hang out with friends and laugh. Once my party was over, I spent the next three months making myself not feel so nervous about being on the field. My sophomore year of soccer season was over, and I did not play that season but was still a part of the team as the manager, which helped in boosting my spirits.

I was asked by my club team if I wanted to play in a Quickfoot tournament, which consists of four players versus four players on a smaller soccer field with a smaller goal. I didn't want to say yes at all until my best friend Sophie talked me into it and said that I would be on her team. After a few days of decision-making, I finally said yes and agreed to play.

The tournament came, and I was so nervous at first, but as the games went on, I became less nervous. I finally felt a little better to play a full game and get back to practicing. The next month, on May 3, 2015, I played my first official full-field soccer game. It was so hard and frustrating for me because I realized I was not the player I was before I was hurt. I wasn't as fast or as quick on the ball, and I was not in shape like I used to be. However, I could tell that I was way smarter on the ball and that was thanks to Coach Erickson, who told me that watching the game of soccer is just as important as playing. I was so mentally full of soccer from watching it for three years that it was frustrating because I wasn't physically there yet. I realized that it would be a long summer of training to get myself back to where I had been.

After a long weekend of soccer, the week had finally come for me to take my driver's test. I was so nervous that I was going to fail and not be able to drive by myself, but there was no reason to be nervous because I easily passed. That's right—better watch the roads because I could drive by myself now. May was such a good month, and I was so excited to carry that on into the summer. And just like that, the summer of 2015 arrived, and my sophomore year of high school was over.

I spent the summer of 2015 training at a high school soccer summer workout and starting a new club soccer team. I trained with my high school team that summer, and it felt so good to be back with the team from the few weeks we had off, and this time I was able to get to work out and play soccer with them. I met three of my other best friends at those summer workouts. Their names were Lauren, Payton, and Evan, and they were upcoming freshmen in high school.

One day after workouts, we wanted to go play soccer, so we went down to the practice turf field. It was way too hot, so we decided to go to the grassy field on the other side of the building. Most of us could drive, so we were all going to drive over there so we didn't have to walk. I was about to get in my car when I saw these three freshman girls just standing there. I asked them if they would like a ride over. They looked at me like they didn't know me well and shouldn't get in the car. I told them it was just on the other side of the school; we weren't going far.

They got in, and I asked them what their names were. We played soccer for a little while, and then the team wanted to grab food together. I told Lauren, Payton, and Evan they could ride with me. They called their moms, and, at first, their moms were hesitant because they had never met me, but Lauren and her mom knew who I was because of my accident. Also, Lauren's mom and my mom grew up together but lost touch over the years. Once their moms said yes, it became an everyday thing, and we hung out on the weekends. That's how they became three of my best friends.

I started a new soccer team that summer, and I was freaking out. My mom kept hearing about this club team called FC Dallas, a well-known organization full of amazing club teams. The team I was going to try out for was based out of Tyler. One of my friends from my high school soccer team named Megan was on the team that was a year younger than the one I planned to try out for. She told me to come to practice with her in Tyler to see if I liked it. Our teams would be practicing together twice a week.

My mom and I drove up to Tyler one night to practice, and I was freaking out because I knew I was still nowhere close to being where I was before I was hurt. I went out to practice, and everyone was so sweet and made me feel like I was a part of the team already. Unfortunately, on the night I went, only a few girls who would be on my team were there, and the coach was unable to be there. I got back in the car after practice and told my mom that I loved it and had never seen a practice like this before. I wanted to go to try-outs next week.

Tryouts came fast, and I was more nervous than ever because Megan wouldn't be there, and I wouldn't know anyone. The coach, Jeremey Bernard, came to meet me, along with the manager. My mom and I explained everything that had happened to me over the past couple of years and how I was looking forward to joining this team.

After that, they asked me, "Do we need to give you a red shirt?" That means no contact during practice.

I said, "No, I'm ready to play." That tryout was one of the hardest practices of my life. We did one-on-one drills where every time the ball taken away from you, you had to run to the other side of the field and back. Let's just say I had to do that a lot, but I never once quit. I kept going even if I was nowhere close to the other girls' soccer and speed abilities. The girls were all nice and excited to have me be part of their team. Over that summer, I worked so hard with both my soccer teams and trained hard to get back to my full potential as an athlete, but I was still lacking.

One day, my mom was talking to someone whose daughter also played soccer, and she trained at this facility that helped her become stronger and faster than she had ever been. It was this conversation that led me to a place I fell in love with called APEC, owned by Bobby Stroupe, in Tyler, Texas.

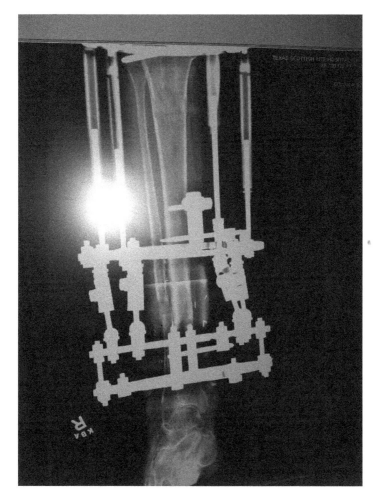

My bone was finally healed and ready for the fixator to come off.

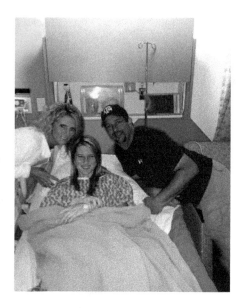

Family picture before the 10th and final surgery to take off my external fixator

Coming home after my last surgery and finally having the fixator off my leg

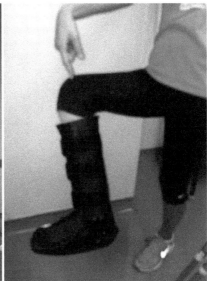

Saying goodbye to my crutches and walking boot

Swimming for the first time in over a year and a half

South Padre trip and a much-needed vacation after the year and a half that my family and I had

I couldn't go back home after the beach trip without seeing Rebekah and Noah.

First day of sophomore year in high school

Riding a bike and putting cleats on for the first time in over a year and a half

October 19, 2014, a day I will forever cherish in my heart—being baptized by my pastor, Bro Danny

Passing my driving permit test and finally starting to feel like a normal teenager again

16th birthday celebration with one of my friends, who I call my twin, Kynlee

A Quickfoot tournament I participated in to begin playing soccer again

Stay off the road—this girl got her driver's license.

Memories from FC Dallas soccer with some of my teammates and Coach Jeremey. They welcomed me with open arms and became like another family to me.

10

But the View Is Great

AS THE SUMMER WAS COMING TO AN END, MY mom contacted the owner of APEC, Bobby Stroupe, and asked if I could come and check the place out. After looking around the building, we signed me up and met the trainer I would be working with one on one, Taylor Nelson-Cook. He was nice and very understanding when I told him I was nervous because of what I had been through. He immediately reassured me that I was in the best hands and that the people at APEC would take the best care of me, working toward getting me back to where I was before my accident.

The first day of my junior year in high school was finally here, and I got to drive myself to school for the very first time. Throughout the fall of my junior year, I was constantly trying to get better and become a better athlete while still trying to keep my grades up. I spent four nights a week in Tyler training at APEC—two nights with Taylor and the other two nights at club soccer practice.

My mom would drive me so that on the way there and home, I could get homework done. I was taking dual credit college class also while in high school and then had after-school soccer practice. I'm not complaining one bit about any of it because although it might have been a lot of hard work, I was able to do all the things I had once taken for granted and never thought I would be able to do again.

When it got closer to soccer season, our head coach started to divide the girls into varsity and junior varsity teams. I was working so hard to get back to where I was before I was hurt and hoping that I would make varsity. However, I did not make varsity that year. At first, I was sad because I was working so hard and all my friends were on varsity. I then remembered that it would give me time to grow and become stronger, and I would be a leader on junior varsity. Coach Adams was my junior varsity coach, and I am so thankful for her. I told myself that even though I made junior varsity, I would still give my coach 110% in everything I did. I was chosen to be one of the captains for my team and was truly blessed that Coach Adams had given me this opportunity.

As the season began, I knew there were tons of people who wanted to watch me play on the field again. I suggested to my mom that we pick a home game and have everyone come to watch that game. My birthday was also that month, so I decided to see if there was a game on that day. There was a game on the night of my actual 17th birthday, so my mom and I decided to start letting everyone know. I told Amber, Mark, and Rebekah. I got a response back from all of them except Rebekah, so I thought she wasn't coming. I remembered that she had promised me she would be at my first game back when I met her. I started to think maybe she was just busy and couldn't make it, so I went on with the next few weeks just hoping this was the case.

The night of my birthday came, and the game was finally here. I saw my nurse Amber in the stands, I saw Mark and Amber in the stands, I saw all my family and friends, but, still, no Rebekah when the game was about to start. Our local news reporter, Lane Luckie with KLTV, was doing a power of prayer segment on their show in a few weeks and thought my story would be an amazing representation of this and a follow-up to my previous interviews. They interviewed me along with my family and friends and videoed some of the game as well. As the game went on, we came out with an 11-0 win, with me scoring one of the first goals. And, guess what--my jersey number was number 11. As we had our talk at the end of the game and took team pictures, I walked over to the stands and started to hug everyone who came. I looked up in the stands, and guess who I saw!

Rebekah and her family were there watching me the whole time. As I was crying, she said, "You didn't think I was going to miss your game, did you? I made a promise to you, and I meant that." I was so happy and thankful that everyone could make it out to my game that night and help me celebrate my 17th birthday.

As the season went on, I continued training at APEC, and it was time for me to start thinking about what I wanted to do for the summer at APEC. Since I had been one-on-one with Taylor for almost a year, he thought it would be a good idea for me to participate in a group class during the summer. I looked at him like he was crazy, but he explained it would be a good way to improve because I was such a competitive person. I told him I would think about it. Then I asked if he would still be my trainer if I did, and he said no.

As my junior year of high school was coming to an end, I finally told Taylor that I would do the group class. This is where I met Kye Heck, my group trainer, and he was awesome. I improved so much that summer and started feeling confident in myself again. Even though all this time had passed since my accident, I was still trying so hard to find all the good in things and where God was leading me because I finally felt like I was seeing the view so clearly from my mountain top.

The minute I started thinking everything looked good and that I had climbed to the top of my mountain and could see the view from the top, I would get knocked down a few steps and have to climb again. In the midst of training all summer at APEC, high school summer workouts, and club soccer practices in Tyler, I found out that my uncle Ricky, who was there the day of my accident, was very sick. Everyone in the family thought it was something he would just get past, but one day my mom called, crying. She said I needed to get my grandpa dressed and bring him to the hospital because my uncle Ricky had passed away.

All I could think about at that moment is that I cannot catch a break when it comes to bad news. We immediately got ready and headed to the hospital. I loved my uncle Ricky so very much, and he would have done anything in this world for his family. I sat in the waiting room, wondering how my family was ever going to get past this. It was one of the hardest summers ever because we had not only lost my uncle Rex and my grandma already, but we had now lost my uncle Ricky too. I felt like my family was getting smaller and smaller.

Toward the end of summer, everything started to get back on track, and it was time to start looking ahead while always holding on to my uncle Ricky in our hearts. It was time to start back-to-school shopping for the upcoming school year. However, this was a bittersweet moment because this was my last school-shopping trip because it was my senior year. I was so ready to start my senior year but also knew this was the year for a lot of last times.

My last first day of high school came and went just like that. I knew I was ready for a good year ahead, and I knew I should soak in every last minute of it. This was also a stressful time because I had to start thinking about college and what I wanted to do with my life.

On January 20, 2017, the four-year anniversary of my accident, I decided that day I wasn't going to be scared of my scar anymore. Most people don't realize that since my accident, I had always been afraid of what others would say or think about the huge scar on my leg. I finally realized it was crazy to feel this way because the true people in my life and the kind people around me shouldn't care what my leg looks like. So, the night before, I told my mom to take a picture of my leg without the compression sleeve I usually wore to cover it.

I was so nervous, but I decided to post it on Facebook the next day because I didn't want kids to be afraid of the way they look or the scars they have. I wanted everyone to know they are beautiful and that it shouldn't matter what other people think. My best friend, Maleah, was with me at school when I decided to post the picture on Facebook. She could tell that I was thinking about backing out of doing it. She told me she was right there with me and that I got this. She said, "Just think of how many people you will inspire to do just the same thing." So, I hit the post button and tears started to come out because I was so nervous. Maleah hugged me and said, "I am so proud of you." If it wasn't for Maleah, I don't think I would have followed through with posting it.

Varsity soccer season came and went like that, and then it was time for prom. Afterward, the rest of the school year felt like it was taking forever, and senioritis was a real thing. I enjoyed every second of high school. The night before the last day, we did our senior prank and went to eat together one last time. The last day flew by, and suddenly, the last bell of the day rang—except, for me, it was the last bell ring I would ever hear. It was a bittersweet day and a last day of school I will never forget.

Graduation was the next day, and before any of us knew it, they were saying, "Class of 2017, you are finally done." High school was one of the hardest times of my life but also one of the best. Being hurt made high school a little more challenging for me the first year or two, but I am so thankful for all my amazing teachers, classmates, all the staff at Hallsville High School, and, last but not least, my parents, who helped me through all the difficult times following my accident.

Today, I am 20 years old, and I can say that I made it to the top of that mountain, and the view is amazing. However, I know there will be many more mountains to climb, but as long as God is by my side, I can climb to the top of every single one of them. Many people ask me nowadays if I could go back to that day knowing I would get hurt, would I have stayed off the ATV? If I am being honest, this has been the toughest six years of my life, but I wouldn't change one thing about January 20, 2013.

I am ashamed to say that if there was ever a time I doubted God, it was at the beginning of this climb. My relationship with God is forever continuing to grow in my life to this day. I was constantly going with sports and school that I never slowed down to take time to learn more about

God. Yes, I said my prayers every night before I went to bed, and my family went to church on Sunday morning, but that still wasn't enough for God.

See, that's the thing about God, you can't just give him a little of you and think that's good enough. You can't just walk through the motion of a relationship with God; you have to show it and apply it. You have to find out what he wants you to learn and do with your relationship with him. God wants every ounce of your heart, and he will give you things to help you realize your relationship with him isn't where it should be. Before my accident, I know I was walking through the motions. I believed in God; I just wasn't where he wanted me to be with him.

It's okay to play sports and do normal kid things and to have busy lifestyles, but when it starts affecting your relationship with God, he will make sure he puts you right back into perspective, where he wants you. I know I will never forget this climb I went on, but I am so looking forward to what lies ahead for me. I'm looking forward to continuing to grow my relationship with God and to tell others the amazing work he has done in my life and, hopefully, help others see the light shine through me.

After I got hurt, the doctors told me this would be one of the longest roads ahead for me and, boy, was this true! I have also realized through all this that everything will happen in God's timing. No matter how bad you might want something right then and there, if God's not ready for you to have it, then it will not happen until his perfect timing. If this hadn't happened to me, I wouldn't have met some of the most amazing people I now have in my life.

Now, I wake up every day and try to live my life to the fullest and make sure to never take anything for granted. I know now that life is so precious and can be taken away from us at any time. Through this whole climb to the top of my mountain, I lost two close family members, and I know they would be so proud to see how far I have come. I know they are going to be right by my side through everything because they are now my guardian angels.

It's hard to be young and have scars because people can be mean. I hope I can help someone, who is my age and struggling with scars, know they are beautiful no matter what someone else says. I know it's hard to hear that and think it's true because I didn't believe it for the longest time. Just know that scar is your story and that you made it through something amazing. I hope I can inspire someone else out there to share their testimony. Small or big everyone has a story, and you might not realize it at the time, but you can always make a difference in someone's life. I hope that I can make a difference in someone's life by telling my story and help them never give up, even when they might have every reason to. I hope that if someone out there is coming face to face with their mountain, I can inspire you to never fear your climb.

Training at APEC with my trainer, Taylor

First day of junior year in high school and first time driving myself to school

Junior Varsity soccer season with some amazing teammates, my co-captain Madi Horne, and, of course, Coach Adams

My 17th birthday home game celebration with friends and family who have followed my story from the beginning and wanted to see me playing again.

Training at APEC during the summer of 2016 with my group and trainer Kye.

Last first day of school picture for my senior year with my best friends, Lauren and Payton.

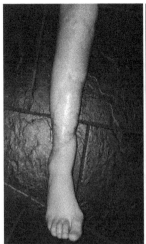 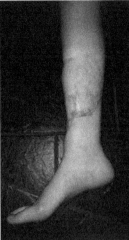 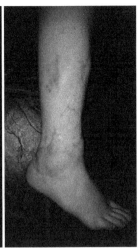

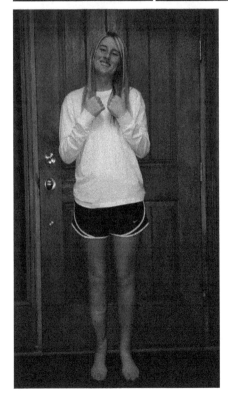

The pictures I posted on Facebook on January 20th, 2017, four years after my accident, showing the scar on my leg for the first time

Varsity soccer season was one to remember with my teammates and coach Erickson because I got to play the sport I love for one last time and...

...we won district champs for the first time in history for our high school girls' soccer program.

Last day of school with my best friend Maleah

Hallsville High School Class of 2017 graduation ceremony

My last ever doctor's visit on June 30th, 2017. I will never ever forget this place.

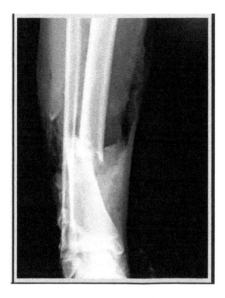

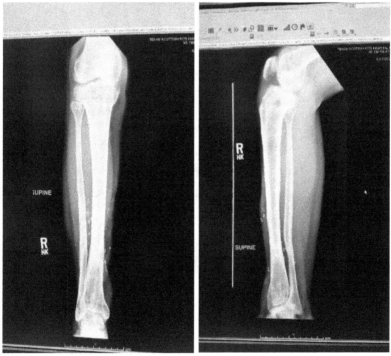

The first picture is from the first x-ray, and the last two pictures are my bone today—perfectly healed with no complications.

Me today, at the age of 20 and capable of doing everything I could before I got hurt and so much more

11

Thank You

THERE ARE SO MANY PEOPLE I WISH I COULD SAY thank you to in person, but this is the next best thing. I want to first start by saying thank you to each one of you who prayed for me and was there throughout this journey with me. I want to also thank you for keeping up with my story and helping me reach the top of this mountain. Without your support and prayers, there's no telling where I would be right now.

I would like to thank every single one of those who took time out of their day to come visit me in Dallas or at my house. Thank you for writing me letters or sending me encouraging messages when I needed them most. Each one of you helped me to never give up because you all gave me a reason to keep fighting until I reached the top of the mountain.

I would like to thank my nurses at both hospitals. I might not have been close to each one of you but know that I thank you for helping me. I still stay in touch with my favorite nurses—Jon, Amber, and Johanna, and I want them to know that I truly am blessed to have had them as my nurses during a time when I needed someone like them in my life. They always knew how to make me smile even when I was in so much pain and always knew the right thing to say at the right moment. Each of them made an impact on my life that I will never forget, and I am blessed to have them in my life to this day.

I would like to thank my amazing doctors because without their hard work, I would not have a leg. Dr. Riccio, Dr. Wimberley, and Dr. Smartt—there will never be enough words in this world for me to tell each one of you how thankful I am for you. I could not have asked for more amazing and caring doctors in this world. Each of you made sure I had the best care every time I had surgery, had to stay in the hospital, or had a doctor appointment. Every time I would get bad news, all of you made sure I understood that you were not done fighting for me to get back to walking and running and that I shouldn't be done fighting either. This journey is over, but I will not forget about you and will visit the hospital again—this time not as a patient.

I would like to also thank Mark and Amber Hapka for reaching out to a stranger to tell me Mark's story when I needed someone to give me light in my life. I was at the beginning of my journey when I first met you, and you have stood by me every step of the way. I am truly blessed to still have you in my life and can't wait until we get to catch up again in person.

I would like to thank Jackson Koster and his family for allowing me to talk to him during a time when he needed to speak to someone going through a similar experience. Jackson, you are one of the strongest people I know, and I hope you realize that you made a huge impact on my life. You made me realize that one of the reasons this accident happened to me was so that I could inspire other people to not give up, like yourself. You healed sooner than me, and because of that, I was able to watch you get back to playing sports. You gave me hope at that time that I would eventually get back to playing soccer.

I want to thank each one of my soccer teammates. Every single one of you helped me in ways that you will never know. I thank each one of the teammates from the team I was on when I first got hurt. Every time I went to a practice or game, you guys made me feel like I was still a part of the team, even though I couldn't play. I want to thank Coach John for standing by me as well and helping me feel at ease in making it through my first Quickfoot soccer tournament.

I want to thank the new club soccer team, FC Dallas, that welcomed me with open arms when I tried out. You guys pushed me during a time when I wanted to quit because I felt like I wasn't good enough to be out on that field anymore. I thank you guys for not letting me give up on the sport my heart loves. I want to thank Coach Jeremey Bernard, who was the coach of my new club team. Thank you for making me feel like I had been a part of the team since the beginning and for pushing me to be a better soccer player and person.

I also want to thank my high school soccer coaches, Coach Adams and Coach Erickson, for everything you have done for me. When I first got released to start playing, Coach Erickson, you never pushed me to get back on that field until I was ready. You taught me so much about the game of soccer, and for that, I will forever be grateful. Coach Adams, I thank you for trusting me to be a captain on the junior varsity team. There will never be enough words to say thank you to each of my coaches and teammates for believing in me and pushing me to be a better athlete and person.

I want to thank each one of the staff members at APEC in Tyler, Texas for pushing me to "be the best me." Taylor, I want to thank you for encouraging me to never give up even when I wanted to. Thank you for pushing me to give it all I had during my workouts, even when my leg was sore or I was tired. I want to thank you for encouraging me to join the class during the summer I worked out at APEC because without you pushing me, I never would have.

Kye, I want to thank you also for pushing me to never give up and to keep believing in myself, even when I didn't think I was as strong or as fast as the other people in my class at APEC. Bobby, I want to thank you for giving me the opportunity to work out at one of the most amazing facilities. Each one of you had a huge impact on the person I am today. I believe in myself even when I feel like I'm not strong enough or good enough because of each of you. APEC will forever hold a very special place in my heart, and I will never forget any of you.

I would like to thank each of my teachers who helped me through this and made sure I was still able to graduate with the classmates I had grown up with. It was tough, balancing school and everything I was going through, but each of you helped me get through it and stay on track. I would like to personally thank Mrs. Howard, who always made sure I was okay and didn't need help with anything, who took time out of her day to make sure I was staying on track for school. Mrs. Howard, you will never realize how much of an impact you had on my life and my high school years. I can never say thank you enough for everything you did for me.

Thank you to Mulberry Springs Baptist Church for everything you did for my family and me during this time. I could not have asked for a better church family. Brother Danny, thank you for always coming to see me during this time and praying over me. Your words always touched my heart, even if I was still confused about my relationship with God at the time of the accident. I will forever and always be thankful to be a part of this amazing church family.

I want to thank one of my best friends, Maleah, who stuck by my side through it all. Maleah, I cannot thank you enough for all those times you stayed right by my side when I was hurt and so nervous about going back to school. You made sure that I was okay during school and made sure I didn't need help. You were literally right beside me when I decided to post the picture of my leg on Facebook. You could tell how scared I was and kept encouraging me and telling me that everything would be okay if I posted it. If you hadn't been there that day, I probably never would have posted it. All of this has brought us closer as friends, and I am forever thankful for you.

I would also like to thank Payton for always pushing me to be a better person. I am thankful to have a friend like you, who always keeps me laughing but, more importantly, helps me continue to grow my relationship with God. I will never take for granted the friendship we have and will have for years to come. Evan, where do I begin? Thank you for constantly making me laugh when I had bad days. I wish I had known you better when I first had my accident because you would have been the one I called to make me laugh on bad days. I know both of you might not have been there when I first had the accident, but I'm truly blessed to have you in my life now. Payton and Evan, I love each of you beyond the moon.

I would like to thank the Battles family for being there for me. Shane, Sheri, Lauren, Kylie, and Emily—I know we weren't close when I was first hurt, but your family kept me in your prayers the whole time. When I first became friends with Lauren, you took me in like another daughter, and I will forever be blessed for that. If there is ever a family I want in my life to help me continue my relationship with God, it is yours. Lauren, our friendship is something I cherish every day and will never take for granted.

Sophie, I want to thank you for also being one of my best friends through this all. You became one of my closest friends about six months before my accident and never once left my side afterward. I am so thankful for you, and you mean the absolute world to me. You could have run away from this friendship the minute I got hurt because we had just become friends, but, no, you stuck by me and made sure I knew I could get through this. Thank you for being one of my best friends, and I can't wait to see what the future holds for our friendship as well.

I would like to thank Heather and James Gee for being there not only for me but also for my parents through all of this. You helped them make sure that everything was taken care of back home while we were in Dallas. You made sure you were there for me if I needed anything. Through my whole ordeal, you became second parents to me and never once made me feel like I wasn't a part of your family. I'm truly blessed and thankful to have you in my life. I can't say thank you enough for everything.

One person for sure that I want to thank is Rebekah. Rebekah, I can never thank you enough for everything you have done for me. I honestly think if it wasn't for you coming into my life at the time you did, I would have chosen the bone graft. I hate that you live in Orlando now because it makes it harder for me to see you often, but I know you are doing amazing things out there. I will forever look up to you, and I hope that I can encourage as many people as you do. I'm blessed to have been a part of so many of your most amazing life moments, and I am blessed that you have been a part of so many of my most amazing life moments. I love you beyond the moon, and thank you for everything you have done for me and continue to do.

I would like to thank Danielle, who might not realize it but helped me more than anyone. She was there for me, made sure no one ever said anything negative about me, and always kept me laughing. Danielle, this accident has made us so much closer than we had ever been. Even though I might have been the one that was hurt, I know just how hard this accident was for you. I hope you realize you are one amazing human being and deserve to have the best life that you can possibly have. I love you beyond the moon and want you to know that no matter what, I am so thankful to have you as my cousin.

I want to thank my grandparents on both sides of my family because there is no bond like a grandchild and a grandparent. I want to thank my BB and Papaw for loving me and helping me through it all. Thank you for always reminding me that God is here for me and that the power of prayer works. I want to thank my Papa for being my rock and my best friend. I want to thank my Mimi, who means the world to me even if she isn't here anymore and who is the number one reason I never gave up through this whole journey. I love each of you more than you will ever realize. You hold a very special place in my heart.

I want to thank my parents for making sure I had the best care in the entire world. I could literally write a book and that would still not be enough for me to tell you how thankful I am for both of you. I know there were days where we just wanted to strangle each other. You both made sure to be at every doctor appointment I had, no matter what. I could go on and on about everything you did for me and continue to do, but I am just going to leave it at this. I love you more than you will ever know, and I am so thankful God gave me parents like you that never left my side. This journey has certainly not only brought us closer to God as a whole but also brought us closer together as a family. Thank you for everything.

Finally, I need to say thank you to God. I know he knows just how thankful I am to have a leg that I can not only walk on but run on as well. I know he wants me to tell others about him and lead them to him. Without him, I know none of this would have been possible. I know that he had his hand over me every step of the way. If this hadn't happened to me, I wouldn't be as close as I am to God. Now, I am nowhere close to perfect, and I still make mistakes, but I know God will never leave my side no matter how much I mess up.

My nurse Johanna from Scottish Rite Hospital.

Amber Hunter Norwood, my night nurse from Children's

Jon Higginbotham, my day nurse from Children's

Maleah Cisneros

Thank You

Payton McVey

Evan Hampton

Lauren Battles

Kylie Battles

Thank You

Emily Battles

Sheri Battles

Sophie Steelman

James, Heather, Trinity, and Cole Gee, along with Sophie Steelman

Tommy and Brenda Cubine or, as I like to call them, BB and Papaw

Joe Taylor or, as I like to call him, Papa

Robert and Angel Cubine, but, to me, they're Dad and Mom

A big thank you to Callie Price for taking my amazing book cover photos. God works in mysterious ways; little did I know that when I asked you to take my photos for the book, I would be gaining such an amazing friend. I am so thankful to now have a friend like you in my life and cannot wait to see what the future holds for us. I know God has amazing plans for you, Callie, and I will always be here to remind you of that.

If you are ever in need of a photographer, you will not be disappointed by Callie's work. Not only does she do amazing work but she is so sweet.

Instagram: calliedawnphotograph
Facebook: Callie Dawn Photography